Preventing
Adolescent
Relapse

D1009201

Foreword by Terence T. Gorski

Preventing Adolescent Relapse

A Guide for Parents, Teachers and Counselors

by
Tammy Bell

Based on the CENAPS Model

Herald/House Independence Press
P.O. Box 390
Independence, MO 64055-0390
1-800-767-8181 or 816/521-3015

Distributed by Herald House/Independence Press
P.O. Box 390
Independence, MO 64051-0390

Library of Congress Cataloging-in-Publication Data

Bell, Tammy L.
Preventing Adolescent Relapse: A Guide for Parents, Teachers, and Counselors/by Tammy L. Bell; based on the CENAPS® model of treatment.
p. cm.
ISBN 0-8309-0571-5:
1. Substance abuse—Relapse—Prevention. 2. Substance abuse—Diagnosis. 3. Teenagers—Substance abuse—Prevention. 4. Adolescence. I. CENAPS Corporation. II. Title.
RJ506. D78B44 1990
616.86.0083—dc20   90-4841

Table of Contents

Foreword

Adolescent relapse is a serious problem facing the field of chemical dependency treatment. The treatment of adolescent chemical dependence is a speciality unto itself. To assume that adolescents who abuse drugs will respond to the same treatment as adults is a serious mistake.

For years treatment centers have become frustrated because techniques that work well with adults often fail to help adolescents. Out of desperation, many counselors have assumed that adolescents who do not respond to treatment, are conduct disorders. As a result, they use harsh confrontation and oppressive legal systems to "force" adolescents into recovery. These techniques produce short-term compliance, but as evidenced by the massive failure rates of adolescent programs, they did not produce long-term sobriety. They failed in the long run.

A systematic approach to the treatment of adolescents who are chemically dependent is desperately needed. This approach must bridge the gap between two extremes. On the one hand many people believe that adolescents who abuse chemicals are psychiatric patients who use alcohol and other drugs to mediate the symptoms of underlying adolescent mental disorders. The other extreme is the belief that adolescent chemical dependency is always a primary physical disease that is genetically inherited and unrelated to psychological and social problems. I believe the truth lies somewhere between these two extremes. For many adolescents who are addicted to drugs there is a strong genetic component that predisposes them to abuse and addiction. There is no denying the recent studies which show that large numbers of adolescents who are chemically dependent also have serious emotional and behavioral problems. What is needed is an approach that integrates treatment techniques from both the chemical dependency field and the adolescent mental health field. This information needs to be tempered with a thorough knowledge of adolescent chemical dependency.

I became excited about adolescent treatment in 1981 when I first met Tammy Bell. She was working as an adolescent therapist at First City Recovery Center in Marietta, Ohio. I was contracted to do in-service training on adult relapse prevention methodologies. Tammy became excited by the notion of relapse prevention but rapidly recognized the limitations that the adult model had when applied to adolescents. She began adapting the model to the specific needs of adolescent patients and, as we talked about these adaptations, our professional relationship began to grow.

It was through my collaboration with Tammy that I became aware of the complex interaction between addiction symptomatology, related mental disorders, and the normal stages of adolescent development. As we worked at adapting the developmental model of recovery and the concept of relapse warning signs in adolescents it became clear that these three different bodies of knowledge could be effectively integrated into a diagnostic and treatment system for adolescents.

As Tammy began applying these methods with adolescents, it became apparent that many adolescents who return to drinking were not relapsing at all; they failed to enter an initial recovery process. Many adolescents were forced into treatment without being given an opportunity to explore their own chemical use and its consequences and make a decision for themselves. Because adolescents lack power in their lives, they are experts at compliance. When the power of their parents, the legal system, and the school system is brought to bear, most adolescents are capable of playing the game. The result is a perfect patient during treatment and a rapid return to chemical use when the adolescent is returned to a less restrictive environment. High relapse rates result.

Tammy was instrumental in developing a way out of this dilemma. By instituting a series of premotivational counseling sessions that actually prepare the adolescent for treatment, the patients she worked with arrived at inpatient facilities voluntarily and ready to participate. As a result the initial resistance was bypassed and the tendency to comply rather than respond to treatment was avoided.

I believe Tammy's book on adolescent relapse prevention is a breakthrough that is much needed for the field. This book integrates in a clear and easy-to-understand way the complex interactions between the symptoms of adolescent chemical addiction, the stages of normal adolescent development, and the presence of adolescent mental disorders in a number of clients. The ideas are sound and comprehensive enough for professionals while being easy enough for most parents to understand.

I strongly recommend this book for all counselors and therapists in dealing with adolescents and their families. I also recommend it for parents who are seriously interested in finding out what they can do to deal effectively with their child's chemical dependency.

Terence T. Gorski
April 1990

Acknowledgments

The experience of organizing this material has taught me that no one writes a book alone. Many people have contributed to this effort in both direct and indirect ways. The people who have contributed most to the completion of this book include the following:

Adolescent program directors and counselors throughout the United States, who shared their ideas, accomplishments, and concerns about their profession;

Every adolescent I have ever worked with, who contributed to my understanding of adolescent treatment;

Jan Smith, for her honest feedback, friendship, and support;

Marjorie Kimmel and Francis DeMarco, for supporting my original concepts and providing the environment, guidance, and friendship I needed to pursue my ideas;

Terence Gorski, for clarifying the recovery and relapse process for chemically dependent adults, for pushing me forward, and for accepting the role of mentor; and

The most significant contributor, who provided me with continuous emotional support, love, and devotion: **my husband, David!**

Tammy L. Bell

Chapter

1

Adolescent Relapse Prevention "The Challenge"

The primary problem that plagues the field of Adolescent Chemical Dependency is that large numbers of previously treated adolescents are not sober. Many treatment professionals believe that relapse goes with the "adolescent territory." They seem convinced that it is almost impossible to keep most of these adolescents sober.

I do not believe this is true; I believe that relapse rates for *recovering* chemically dependent adolescents are *not* astronomical. I do agree, however, that we don't have very many adolescents in recovery. I believe the reason for this is that most of the chemically dependent adolescents who have been treated **never entered** recovery—**they really never got sober.**

These youngsters practice controlled abstinence which has been forced on them by admitting them to inpatient treatment programs. Most of these adolescents have not yet accepted the fact of their addiction. They have no real intention of staying sober and, therefore, never really enter the recovery process.

They may learn to "talk the talk" of recovery but they don't "walk the walk." And in their hearts and minds they believe they will return to using chemicals. They are simply trying to relieve the family stress and survive the inpatient treatment experience.

I believe that if people who work with chemically dependent adolescents understood two very important fundamental concepts they would see addiction recovery rates in adolescents improve significantly.

1. *Pretreatment issues.* It is critically important that we understand the **pretreatment component of recovery.** "Pretreatment" adolescents believe they are "social" drinkers or "recreational" drug users who are in control of their use of chemicals. The only problem they believe they have is that they have been caught using alcohol or drugs and are being punished by adults who "really don't understand what's going on."

Harsh confrontation does not move adolescents out of pretreatment. It only forces a state of "compliance" that drives them deeper into this stage of their disease. When we as professionals understand how to recognize and address pretreatment issues, we will see a significant increase in the percentage of adolescents that actually get into the recovery process.

2. *Adolescent development issues.* Many adolescent chemical dependency treatment programs, as well as the nature of Twelve-Step programs, don't allow for and often directly threaten the normal adolescent developmental tasks that **all adolescents,** chemically dependent or not, **are internally driven to complete.**

The idea that adolescents should simply accept adult wisdom, turn their lives over to a sponsor, and follow a Twelve-Step program is often unrealistic. Directives such as "sit down and shut up, listen and don't talk, and just do what I tell you" conflict with the fundamental developmental tasks that an adolescent must accomplish in order to become an adult. This does not mean that adolescents shouldn't do these things in recovery. It does mean that many treatment providers do not understand how to introduce these concepts or how to use the motivational techniques that will lead adolescents into recovery.

Adolescents must come to understand *on their own,* and not because we told them, that they are chemically dependent. They must come to believe that they cannot control their alcohol and drug use and that they need to live lives of abstinence and work a Twelve-Step program.

Adolescents must come to understand **on their own,** *and not because we told them, that they are chemically dependent.*

This approach works, and these things can and do happen with adolescents. I have been successful in treating chemically dependent adolescents using this approach, and I believe that my success with adolescents based on this model are a result of (1) understanding adolescent development, and (2) developing a protocol to resolve pretreatment issues.

This book presents information that indicates it is necessary to treat chemically dependent adolescents and get them into the recovery process "the first time around." This book also contains information about relapse that specifically applies to preventing relapse in previously treated adolescents, as well as interrupting the relapse process in adolescents who are currently experiencing it. First and foremost, it addresses the primary problem that confronts the field of adolescent chemical dependency, which is that adolescents are not getting sober.

Father Joseph Martin, a highly respected veteran in the addiction treatment profession, has said, "The definition of insanity is doing the same thing over and over again and expecting a different outcome." In the decade of the 1980s, in which we have seen a proliferation of programs treating chemically dependent adolescents, we have consistently experienced low and sometimes nonexisting recovery rates with this population. As a profession, we blamed the patients and changed nothing about our treatment approach, regardless of how many failures we saw.

This book is not meant to attack. It is meant to increase the number of chemically dependent adolescents who ultimately recover. Recovery must become more than an empty promise. If relapse is our only realistic expectation, we are failing the adolescents who need our help. We can do better for them, and this book will show you how. It is designed to give you insight, understanding, and useful tools to get chemically dependent adolescents into recovery and to help them develop effective relapse prevention planning once they are there.

Chapter

2

Adolescents and Chemicals

These interlocking circles represent the three major knowledge bases we must understand and which overlap in treating chemically dependent adolescents.

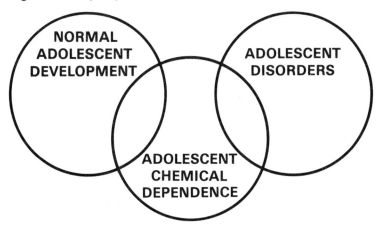

This is the most effective way to treat this population. We cannot focus on just one aspect of chemically dependent adolescents and fail to look at the entire picture.

First we must understand the principles of *normal adolescent development* that apply to all adolescents whether they are chemically dependent or not. Recovering adolescents and people who work with them need to know what the average adolescent should be able to do at a certain age in order to recognize any behaviors that are abnormal.

This has been a problem in the chemical dependency field. Some persons who are trying to treat chemically dependent adolescents have little or no understanding of adolescence. They say, "We have a little adult here, and what we are going to do is to treat him in an adult system, with adult techniques, and make him shape up or ship out." And that doesn't work.

In order to understand adolescent chemical dependency we must recognize its relationship to both normal adolescent behavior and other adolescent disorders.

Adolescents are not simply "little adults." They are people who are somewhere between childhood and adulthood. They have some specific needs that must be met if they are going to benefit from treatment. We need to know, therefore, in detail, what's *normal.* As adolescent care givers, we need to ask, "What should I expect? What should I be looking for? How can I determine which behaviors are normal and which are adolescent disorders or behaviors related to chemical use?"

The second area of focus in helping chemically dependent adolescents is **adolescent disorders.** What are the most common adolescent disorders that plague chemically dependent adolescents? What may be affecting them other than chemical dependency? A chemically dependent adolescent who has a coexisting untreated psychiatric disorder may not be able to remain functional enough to work a recovery program. Therefore, we must be able to recognize and treat common disorders to help chemically dependent adolescents avoid relapse.

Our third area of focus is **adolescent chemical dependence.** How do we differentiate between experimentation, drug or alcohol abuse, and chemical dependency? We know that the tools for evaluating adult chemical dependency do not apply very well to adolescents as they are very behaviorally weighted. They tend to evaluate a great deal based on the person's behavior. Because a large part of normal adolescence is "childlike" behavior, using adult instruments to evaluate adolescents often provides inaccurate results. The tools I am presenting have been designed for evaluating adolescent chemical dependency and provide a far more accurate assessment of a child's chemical use.

Adolescents and Chemicals

Before we focus on chemically dependent adolescents let's examine what "normal" teenagers are doing. If "normal" means how the *majority* of people behave, then what is normal adolescent chemical use in America? The National Institute of Alcoholism and Alcohol Abuse (NIAAA) prepared a report entitled "NIAAA Adolescent Report, 1987" based on statistics the NIAAA compiled from a variety of research projects. These data were obtained by surveying schools and other places that provide services and activities for teenagers and are not representative of chemically dependent adolescents alone.

The following is a summary of the NIAAA report of "normal" adolescent chemical use in America today.

1. *Alcohol remains the most widely used drug among adolescents.* It is not marijuana nor the "harder" drugs. Given a choice, adolescents still prefer to use alcohol over and above other drugs.

2. *Alcohol use by adolescents has increased 4.5 percent in the last ten years.* All the "stop using drugs" pro-

grams we have launched have not deterred adolescents from drinking. This research shows that marijuana use did go down slightly, but it also indicates that alcohol use by adolescents is clearly on an incline. This says to me that our "Just Say No" programs haven't worked.

One reason for this is that stopping adolescents from using chemicals is a little more complicated than just saying "No!" Although I welcome these efforts from the White House and others, that approach isn't the best or the most effective for adolescents. The "Just Say No" program has given us mixed messages. Have you noticed that the focus is rarely on alcohol? All the commercials we see warn against "drugs": "Don't do crack" and "Don't do cocaine."

For example, Bruce Willis (of "Moonlighting") was one of the national chairfolk for the "Just Say No" campaign and he's made many of their commercials. In one he said, "Don't do crack! Just say 'No!'" The focus of another was: "Don't do cocaine! Just say 'No!'" At the same time Bruce regularly appeared in advertisements for wine coolers. So what's the message that adolescents and parents are getting? That drinking alcohol is okay; that alcohol is not a "drug"—and it is!

At the same time that Bruce is standing there in front of many teenagers who idolize him saying, "Don't do drugs," he's also telling them that it's romantic, "cool," and "macho" to drink alcohol. I'm sure that this is not due to any maliciousness on Bruce's part; he probably doesn't even understand the connection.

Parents are also misled by this. Some parents I've interviewed and told that their adolescent is an alcoholic have said, "Well, thank God he's not on drugs!" These parents tell their children, "Honey, we don't care if you drink; just don't smoke pot. Don't get into drugs!" And often they even support their adolescent's drinking. They say, "If you want a beer, have it here at home."

3. *Moderate to heavy use of alcohol is directly associated with use of marijuana and other illicit drugs.* We have always believed that, but for a long time we didn't have any research to back it up. Now we do. This report shows that 36 percent of moderate drinkers and 63 percent of heavy drinkers report using marijuana or other drugs during the past month compared to only 7 percent of infrequent drinkers.

Alcohol is clearly a "gateway" drug to "harder" drugs. Adolescents who start to use alcohol regularly often go on to using marijuana and to harder drugs as well.

4. *About 4.6 million adolescents are harmfully involved with alcohol and 5 percent of those adolescents drink daily.* Based on this research, of the approximately 22 million adolescents in the United States, 4.6 million are "harmfully involved" with alcohol. This means they are paying considerably through the adverse consequences of drinking. They are either tied into the court system, have serious family problems, have been kicked out of school, or suffer other serious consequences of drinking.

5. *Adolescents are drinking at increasingly younger ages. The first drink has dropped two grade levels, from the ninth to the seventh.* In 1975 most adolescents usually experimented with alcohol in the ninth grade. These data indicate that by 1985, most adolescents were having their first drink in the seventh grade. This means they are experimenting much earlier.

6. *The mean age for the first drink in this country is twelve years and three months, and it is thirteen and four months for the first marijuana use.* Remember, these are not adolescents in treatment programs that we are focusing on here. This is the average among our "normal" adolescents.

7. *Four percent of ten- to thirteen-year-old adolescents are regular drinkers.* That one shocked me. I wasn't

expecting that statistic to be so high. For this research, "regular drinker" is defined as one who drinks at least once a month. And 8 percent of the 4 percent of adolescents in this age-group reported that they drank alcohol on four or more occasions during the preceding month, and with no differences between boys and girls.

This is significant because at present there are a higher proportion of males than females in substance abuse programs. The ratio is two boys to each girl. Until recently, girls didn't drink as often as boys or in the same quantity. That's not true for the children coming up behind the youngsters who are in treatment now. "Pre-teen-age" girls are drinking as much and as often as the boys in that age-group.

8. *The perception of alcohol use among peers is believed to be high among fourth through twelfth graders.* As many as 35 percent of fourth graders feel peer pressure to drink. This particular piece of research was done by the *Weekly Reader!*

The drinking patterns among our adolescents are changing and they are not getting better. Some of the young children who are discovering alcohol now are going to be chemically dependent adolescents in the near future. Based on this research, we can make some guesses and projections about the population of chemically dependent young people with whom we will be working next: children under the age of twelve today.

In light of these scary statistics, the questions we need to ask are: "What do we have to do to prepare for treating chemically dependent adolescents in the future? What does or doesn't work. What will we need to do differently?"

1. First, all of the efforts of our "national war on drugs" have failed for many reasons, one of which is that they rarely include alcohol. Adolescents need to be reminded that alcohol in any form—beer, wine coolers, or chocolate creme liqueur—is still a *drug.*

2. Adolescent alcohol use *does* lead to using other drugs, and this isn't just based on a hunch or because that's what we see all the time. The research bears this out, and adolescents, parents, and teachers need to know about this.

3. Adolescents are going to need help at an earlier age. Chemically dependent adolescent patients are getting younger by the day. Four or five years from now, counselors will need to understand *preadolescent* development issues to treat these children effectively.

4. Girls are experimenting with drinking as much as boys, so just as many girls as boys are going to be in trouble and have problems that need to be diagnosed and treated.

5. Clearly, more time needs to be spent on alcohol and drug use prevention programs in schools and in the very lowest grades. If fourth graders are already under peer pressure to drink, it's a little late to start prevention education there. Still, some primary school teachers are opposed to having this information brought to first, second, and third graders because, "After all, these children are so innocent!"

Why Do Adolescents Drink and Use Drugs?

1. *Our society is drug-oriented.* Adolescents are bombarded by television programs and commercials that promote drug use. They receive messages which suggest: "You should never have to feel bad about anything. If you have a headache, allergy, hemorrhoids, arthritis—you name it—you ought to be taking some chemical for it."

It's the same in the average household. In the homes where many of us grew up, as soon as someone sneezed, Mom went to the drug cabinet to get something for it. And she was considered a good mother for doing that.

2. *Adolescents relate to a drug-using subculture.* This includes many members of "heavy metal" rock bands and other popular personalities in the music and entertainment

business. Lyrics of songs and themes of films and TV programs often are slanted toward drug use. Many chemically dependent adolescents have parents with the same disease who are still very much entrenched in the sixties drug subculture. Sometimes parents and adolescents drink and use drugs together.

3. **Genetic influence is a factor.** Based on the high rate of chemical dependency that comes from the same families, we can't argue with this fact. Research shows that liver metabolism problems are prevalent in people who are chemically dependent. Other research done on brain wave activity and deficiences of endorphins (naturally occurring chemicals produced by the brain) in alcoholics and chemically dependent people strongly supports the fact that there is a genetic link.

4. **Family dysfunction.** Many adolescents today come from alcoholic or chemical-abusing families. Others frequently come from homes with some other dysfunction, and they drink or drug to escape.

5. **Lack of meaningful contribution.** There is nothing productive for many adolescents to be involved in in this society. They have no meaningful role in family or the community. Adolescence is a fairly new phenomenon. At one time in this country, as in most other societies, people went from childhood to adulthood. There was no "stage of adolescence" as such; there was a "rite of passage." At thirteen a person was a young man or woman. Now that's gone; adolescents are children who are no longer children but also are not adults. They are expected to "act their age," but there is no clear definition of what that means.

In past years, by the age of twelve or thirteen people were expected to go out and work, to be involved in society, contribute to the support of the home, and take care of themselves. What meaningful thing are adolescents expected or able to provide for their country, their household, or even for themselves today? Nothing—or at least, not much for most adolescents.

Young people who are developing the same intellectual capability that adults have also have the same need to feel productive, to feel needed, to feel important. These needs are met for most adults by their work. When we ask an adult to "tell me about yourself" they say, "I'm George and I work at...," right? What do adolescents say? When a sixteen-, seventeen-, or eighteen-year-old says, "Hi, I'm Brenda and I go to such and such a high school," she recognizes that this means very little. Adolescents know it means that they don't contribute anything.

Work done by psychologist Stephen Glenn, among others, shows that getting adolescents involved in meaningful work—not just tasks around the house but actual work that contributes to the overall good of the family and society—helps them to have a greater sense of self-respect and self-esteem. These adolescents seem to develop stronger values.

Like adults, adolescents need to see an end product in what they do. They need to feel important, and often in this society they cannot. Parents and other adults expect them to act responsibly; yet many times adolescents have nothing to be responsible for, and they recognize this. For this reason, some adolescents find the adolescent years to be the most confusing, frustrating, and miserable period of their lives. Drinking and using drugs offer a temporary escape, though rarely without devastating consequences.

6. *Adolescence is an uncomfortable and often painful time of life.* I can think back on my own adolescence. When I was fourteen or fifteen years old, I remember people asking me, "Tammy, why are you sitting there depressed? What is wrong with you? These are the best years of your life!" That's enough to cause someone that age to commit suicide! They were telling me it went downhill from there: it was going to get worse!

23

In thinking back on their own adolescence, few adults would want to repeat it. Adolescents are not in a comfortable phase of life. We adults need to remember that, particularly at times when an adolescent is really frustrating us. Sometimes we need to take a deep breath, close our eyes for a minute, jump back into our own shoes at that child's age, and think about how we would respond to how we are treating them.

Because chemical use among adolescents is so widespread, and because we have seen such appallingly poor results in treating chemically dependent adolescents to date it is clearly time to rethink our traditional approach and to ask what's wrong. Given the magnitude of the problem, the tidal wave of chemically dependent adolescents on the horizon of the nineties, we must develop solutions that work. To do this we need to understand what makes chemically dependent adolescents difficult to treat and design approaches to treating them that address these issues.

Why Are Chemically Dependent
Adolescents Difficult to Treat?

There are four major reasons why chemically dependent adolescents are more difficult to treat than the adult population with whom we work. The following four things that adolescents experience cause problems for us and make treating their chemical dependency difficult.

1. *Normal adolescent developmental issues.* These include egocentric-enabling family systems; lack of life experience—not knowing what "normal" is; a "nothing-to-lose" attitude based on the myth of immortality; and an inner drive for autonomy which compels adolescents to challenge adults. These are normal adolescent development issues that are important for all adolescents to work through during these years, but which foster attitudes that are a direct affront to most adults.

24

2. *Chemical dependency.* Chemically dependent people of any age are not easy to be around, let alone treat. Alcoholics and drug-addicted people are not the easiest patients to deal with or to cope with. Often, these adolescents are acting out behaviorally the direct results of their chemical addiction and what chemicals have done to them.

3. *Multiple diagnosis.* Many chemically dependent adolescents suffer from dual or multiple disorders. Often, these problems interfere with the adolescents' ability to work a recovery program. Psychiatrist Bill Stone says, "*All* chemically dependent adolescents have a dual diagnosis. They are chemical dependent and they are adolescent."

4. *Dysfunctional families.* Many chemically dependent adolescents have divorce or step-family issues, lack of positive role models, and drug and alcohol abuse in the home, to name just a few problems associated with coming from dysfunctional families.

These are the four major factors which chemically dependent adolescents experience. That they are not in control of these factors makes working with them difficult—and none of these factors are easy to deal with. But there's more to consider: It isn't all *them.* We tend to focus on what these terrible adolescents do to *us* that makes our jobs of helping them so hard, but it isn't all *them.*

In any relationship that isn't working, it takes two to make it and it takes two to break it. That is true in a marriage and it is true in therapy. If something isn't working effectively with an adolescent, it *may* be the adolescent, but it isn't *always* the adolescent. We have to look at ourselves sometimes.

Let's consider what *we* often do to adolescents that makes them difficult to treat. These are called iatrogenic factors, meaning physician-induced illnesses. An example of this is what happens when a surgeon doesn't "scrub" adequately before surgery and then takes out someone's gall bladder. If the person develops an infection as a result of that operation, the infection is an iatrogenic or physician-induced illness. Sometimes adolescents have therapeutic-induced problems that are caused by their therapist, counselor, social service worker, probation officer, or teacher.

Some of the things that professional helpers do that contribute to making adolescents difficult to treat include the following:

Sometimes adolescents have therapeutic-induced problems that are caused by their therapist, counselor, social worker, probation officer, or teacher.

---

1. *Applying adult criteria to adolescents.* Sometimes we expect adolescents to act as if they are twenty-five or thirty, and when they don't, we are angry. It isn't realistic to expect fifteen-year-olds to act like they are adults. We should be very disappointed and concerned about them if they do because it means they are playing a game.

2. *Misdiagnosing adolescents.* Many adolescents in various treatment systems have either been inadequately or under diagnosed. A chemically dependent adolescent may also be suffering from depression, an eating disorder, or a learning disability. Then when the adolescent acts out because he or she is not being treated for coexisting problems, we respond with discipline rather than appropriate therapy.

3. *Having unrealistic expectations regarding success.* What is the definition of "success" for chemically dependent adolescents who go into treatment? Is it that they will leave treatment chemically free, abstain from chemicals for the rest of their lives, get a job, get married, have a family,

and send their youngsters to college? Is that the definition of successful treatment?

Some definitions of success are unrealistic for adolescents. Suppose a boy is completely dysfunctional and comes from an unhealthy family system. If on leaving treatment that child understands that drugs are a problem for him and that he will always need help with drugs, and he then goes about his life trying and working toward recovery, *that* is a major accomplishment. And if that adolescent relapses into use of the drugs, it does not mean that he has failed. We have to look at where he started. It is reasonable to have higher expectations for a very functional adolescent coming from a healthy family system, but success cannot be defined the same for each child. That's unrealistic.

When I go into treatment centers and ask people, "What is your definition of success? How do you know you have been successful with a chemically dependent adolescent?" most often they say, "Success is when the adolescent goes into recovery, and never uses drugs again."

My response to that is, "Wow! How many times has that happened to you?"

4. *Standardized treatment for all adolescents.* I call these "canned" treatment plans. For example, the treatment plan for a thirteen-year-old girl who is an incest survivor is the same as the treatment plan for a seventeen-year-old boy who is depressed. In many treatment programs I see treatment plans written up that are identical for every adolescent on the unit! Age-appropriate and problem-focused treatment plans are what we should see.

Thirteen-year-olds should not have the same things in their treatment plan as seventeen-year-olds. Girls should not always have the same things in their treatment plans as boys do. Most adolescents have difficult issues. Adolescent issues are not generic: they are widely varied. Each adolescent comes from varying experiences, is at a different age, and treatment plans should reflect this. When all treatment plans look the same, the professional helper is not spending enough time giving thought to how to reach *individual* adolescents.

5. ***Sending mixed messages to adolescents.*** These mixed messages include things like *telling* adolescents to "act like an adult" and then *treating* them like children. Or saying, "This is a *disease,* and since you have been *bad,* you will wear your pajamas all day." I call this "pajama therapy." Calling chemical dependency a disease and then treating it like a social problem is sending an inconsistent message to adolescents.

In some treatment programs, adolescents are punished in humiliating ways for not saying the right thing in group. One adolescent reported that he had been told to wear a bathing suit to group "to get in touch with himself." When he refused to do this, he experienced all kinds of consequences. Chemical dependency is a disease, and it should be treated as a disease. When adolescents are punished for not responding to treatment, they are being told that chemical dependency is a social problem. Whether it's harsh restrictions or physical abuse, or even using cigarettes, etc., for a reward system, these methods all reinforce the notion that a treatment center is a penal institution for "bad" people. It smacks of prison to me and it hasn't been very effective.

6. ***When all else fails, blame the child.*** Sometimes when professionals aren't successful with all that they know how to do, they decide, "This child just can't be helped." I've spent a lot of time reading, studying, and talking to other adolescent treatment professionals, and from this I've learned that I certainly don't have all the answers. There is still much about chemically dependent adolescents that I don't understand. Yet what do some counselors do when chemically dependent adolescents don't get well? I know because I have done it.

If an adolescent was not responding to treatment, I would decide, "We just can't help this one." I didn't say, "I must be missing something here. Either I don't have enough training or knowledge, or I've gotten started on the wrong foot, or I have taken the wrong approach." How often does the therapist take responsibility when an adolescent doesn't respond to treatment?

Professional helpers need to be willing to take an honest and searching moral inventory at times and say, "I'm a human being who doesn't have all the answers, and I make mistakes. And sometimes when I'm having problems with an adolescent, it is my fault—or it is our program." No one has all the answers, and no one can work with every chemically dependent adolescent that comes along. Anyone can run into personality conflicts from time to time, or program limitations, and it's OK to admit this. Not to admit this and always blame the adolescent is denial.

7. *Some chemically dependent adolescents have more than one problem.* Adolescents who are conduct disordered and chemically dependent, for example, pose major problems in treatment. But most of these principles still apply to them as well. A criminal will respond better if he's treated with respect. This is true for adult criminals and it is true for troubled adolescents.

Counselors need to gain a thorough understanding of adolescent development and adolescent disorders that complicate treatment of chemically dependent adolescents. It is important to dispel many of the myths about chemically dependent youth that have created prejudice in the past. Adolescents need to know that they are neither "crazy" nor "bad" just because they are chemically dependent.

The CATOR Study

To better understand the profile of chemically dependent adolescents, let's review a study conducted by the Chemical

Abuse Treatment Outcome Registry (CATOR). This study surveyed 2,424 adolescents who were admitted to various in-patient treatment programs throughout the country. Some of the findings in this study may surprise you. The population in this study may not be representative of all chemically dependent adolescents as they are primarily white, middle-income (have the financial means to obtain treatment) males. Economically disadvantaged, minority ethnic groups, and female patients are underrepresented.

Also, this study shows an overlap in statistics because the adolescents were instructed to check all answers that applied to them, and some may have checked more than one response in a given category.

Gender of chemically dependent adolescents. CATOR found that the current adolescent male-to-female ratio in chemically dependent treatment programs is two to one, which is about the same as the current adult population in chemical dependency inpatient treatment. Based on trends of chemical use among adolescents, we can expect this ratio to change to equal numbers of boys and girls in treatment during the next decade.

Behavior problems at school. Twenty-six percent of these adolescents had no school-related problems. Seventy-four percent had been referred to the dean or principal for counseling. Fifty-eight percent had been suspended, and 14 percent had been expelled.

Learning disabilities. Of the adolescents surveyed, 17 to 24 percent were diagnosed as learning disabled (L.D.). Even considering the overlap in these statistics, this is significant. At least one-fourth of the adolescents we are dealing with need to be evaluated and have treatment plans addressing their learning limitations.

Chemical dependency treatment involves a great deal of education. We have to be concerned about the level of comprehension of children with learning disabilities. How can they get into a recovery program if they can't read the "Big Book" of AA, NA's *Basic Text,* or understand the Twelve Steps? How much of the addiction information that we give them do L.D. adolescents understand, particularly if they are being taught with materials and in classes designed for adults?

If we do not evaluate and work with these adolescents in special ways, they will not receive the information or skills necessary to get and stay sober. We need people trained to evaluate L.D. who can work with these children—and this applies no matter what the adolescent's problem is. It doesn't have to be substance abuse. If this resource is not available, even a very well-designed program will have limited impact.

Legal problems. Nineteen percent of the adolescents in these programs had no legal problems, meaning they had never been arrested. Fifty-nine percent had been arrested once. Does this come as a surprise? Many people would expect 100 percent. Forty percent of the adolescents had minor consequences, which means they received a reprimand or were put on probation.

Although a large number of juvenile delinquents are chemically dependent, most chemically dependent adolescents are not juvenile delinquents.

Thirty-seven percent of those arrested were arrested for misdemeanors and 21 percent for status offenses (behaviors that are not illegal for adults but considered offenses for adolescents, such as curfew violations or drinking alcohol). Sixteen percent of the adolescents reported they had been arrested for felonies.

Only 23 percent of these adolescents had suffered severe consequences from legal problems. Although a large number of juvenile delinquents are chemically dependent, most chemically dependent adolescents are not juvenile delinquents.

Medical care utilization. Fifteen percent of the adolescents coming into treatment had been in an inpatient facility in the last year for physical reasons. That's high for this predominately healthy population. Thirty-two percent had been treated in an emergency room for illness or injury and 5 percent for drug overdose.

Thirteen percent of these youngsters had been in outpatient treatment with a psychologist or psychiatrist and 9 percent had been hospitalized for psychiatric problems. Thirty-two percent had already been in inpatient treatment for chemical dependency.

When we look at a medical utilization history like this, on a population that's in the healthiest years of their lives, what does it tell us? One thing is that we should be receiving a much higher percentage of referrals from the medical community; however, when physicians and nurses don't recognize the symptoms, there's no help offered for the child's chemical dependency.

Depression. This is something we really need to pay attention to. Less than 31 percent of the adolescents in this study were *not* suffering from any depression. Sixty-nine percent had mild to moderate depression. That's high. So, like L.D., depression is also a common dual-diagnosis experienced in chemically dependent adolescents.

Suicidal tendencies. Fifty-nine percent of the adolescents had no history of suicidal tendencies. Thirty-eight percent had experienced suicidal ideation, and 18 percent reported having made a recent suicide attempt. These are also high numbers. We have to take suicide threats by adolescents seriously because many of them are carried out.

Sometimes we get complacent and say, "This kid's just doing this for attention." Some of them are; however, we don't know *which* ones and we can't pretend to know. Some adolescents who set up a suicide situation for attention go too far and kill themselves accidentally. So when adolescents are talking suicide or are depressed, we must take this seriously. We have to evaluate them and provide safeguards.

Some adolescents who set up a suicide situation for attention go too far and kill themselves accidentally.

Even when attempts have been made before which have been obvious efforts to gain attention, the child may succeed the next time and go a step too far, either on purpose or by accident.

Physical abuse. Forty-one percent of these adolescents have been physically abused by one or both parents. Physical abuse consists of physical beatings with hands or objects that are outside the range of normal discipline with respect to frequency and intensity. Physical abuse in this society does not include an occasional spanking by adults who are in control of themselves and who do not inflict severe pain, physical marking, or tissue damage.

Physical abuse includes actions by adults who are out of control such as beating, kicking, punching, slapping, pulling hair, biting, or otherwise striking out at a child with either intentional or accidental rage. Such physical abuse often causes bruises, burns, cuts, or welts on the child's body. Chronic, frequent, and repetitive spankings or other forms of physical punishment or restraint (locking or tying up) are all forms of physical abuse.

33

Sexual abuse. Forty-eight percent of the females in this study and 9 percent of the males reported having been sexually abused. That's nearly half of the females and it is three to four times higher than for the general population.

Sexual abuse includes touching, stroking, or manipulating a child or adolescent's sexual organs or forcing or convincing a child or adolescent to do these things to someone else's body. Sexual abuse also includes participating in any sexually oriented activity involving minors.

Sexual abuse may be initiated by complete strangers or neighbors, but most often it is the child's own relatives, siblings, or parents who subject them to sexual abuse.

Children or adolescents who are victims of physical and sexual abuse often experience Post Traumatic Stress Disorder (PTSD). PTSD results from experiencing a frightening and/or stressful event that compromises the victim's personal integrity or is a perceived or real threat to survival. PTSD affects children in a variety of ways such as causing disturbing dreams and nightmares, acting out behavior, difficulty in developing trust, and trouble remembering childhood events. PTSD is explained more fully in chapter 4, "Common Adolescent Disorders."

Physically and sexually abused children who do not receive intervention and treatment often become abusive to their children and the cycle continues. Adolescents who have been abused must be identified in treatment. Untreated PTSD will continue to interfere with their attempts at recovery, making it difficult for them to achieve and maintain long-term sobriety.

Average age of the first chemical use. The average age for first use of alcohol was twelve years and age thirteen for first use of marijuana. Thirty-one percent of the adolescents surveyed reported they had used with their parents. That's nearly one third!

Excessive use of alcohol and drugs by a family

member. Fifty-seven percent of these adolescents had at least one alcohol-abusing member in the family, and 37 percent had at least one drug-abusing member.

Physically and sexually abused children who do not receive intervention and treatment often become abusive to their children and the cycle continues.

We must do more for the families of these young people. Families of chemically dependent adolescents need to be assessed, evaluated, and confronted about their own chemical use. Many parents take the position that treatment is a dumping ground. "If you just fix this kid everything in this house will be fine. This kid's the problem."

When we take these adolescents into treatment they become convinced that they are responsible for the problems of the family. This is generally not the case, but that is the message we give adolescents who are brought into treatment and their families are left out.

We need to mandate that parents attend certain classes and evaluation sessions. It's that simple. We have to bring in the adolescent's parents and evaluate their chemical use as well. We know that at least 57 percent of them are involved in chemicals or are chemically dependent themselves. If they don't get treatment along with their adolescent, the chances of their child relapsing is very high.

When I ask treatment center personnel why they are not evaluating the parents' chemical use they say, "Because it would make them mad. They might take their adolescent out of here." This sounds a bit codependent to me. We can't hide in the family denial system and endorse this kind of behavior.

We need to say, "Look, Mom, based on what you're saying to me here, it looks to me like you need to be evaluated for chemical dependency. You're definitely not a social drinker. It's gone beyond that. And we've got your adolescent here, and we're treating her for chemical dependency, and you need to understand there's a genetic influence to this disease. If we're going to be successful with your child, we need your cooperation. And cooperation means that you too may need to be in some form of counseling or treatment."

It's very difficult sometimes to get families involved in treatment. But we have to tell parents, "This is what we need from you in order to help your child. Now while you're here, let me set up an appointment to evaluate your alcohol and drug use." We need to establish a policy that it's going to be mandatory for all parents if they are to be involved with their adolescent's treatment. If the parents are chemically dependent, they need to get involved in treatment for themselves. And, yes, some folks will get angry about this.

If the parents are chemically dependent, they need to get involved in treatment for themselves.

If we have a nonparticipatory parent or a really dysfunctional family, we may have to talk to a judge about judicial pressure. I know of adolescents who have said, "Please, don't send me home. I want to stay here." We should be evaluating that family and finding out if that adolescent is right. For instance, is it in the best interest of an adolescent who is chemically dependent to send him back to a chemical using famly where he's being abused? No. Not unless there is family intervention and treatment.

When parents are abusing their adolescents or sabotaging their treatment, we need to advocate for these adolescents where possible and provide alternative living arrangements. One approach is to set up foster homes with people who are recovering from chemical dependency themselves, who have been sober a long time, and have a fairly healthy family system.

Sometimes we, as helping professionals, let parents take advantage of us. We take the position, "We're helpless, and we can't change it." And that's not the way it has to be. We can do more with these families; when parents refuse to be part of the recovery process, we must look for and apply leverage with them wherever possible.

At the very least, we should ask that families not make alcohol and drugs available in the home while their adolescent is in early recovery. This does not mean that they can't have liquor in their homes for the rest of their lives. It's as if we have a young child who is diabetic: we don't fill the house with sweets and walk off and leave the child there. I ask parents to "show your adolescent the same consideration you would show with any other illness with respect to what you have available in your home."

If they think that's a real inconvenience then they are not seeing chemical dependency as a disease. And if that's such an inconvenience, then they're more than social drinkers. A social drinker would say, "Let's get rid of all our alcohol. I'm not going to do anything to jeopardize my youngster! No problem."

Recovery status. This data is based on surveys of attendance in sobriety support groups after release from treatment. Of adolescents who had multiple relapses, 65 percent reported that they did not attend AA/NA and aftercare support groups after leaving treatment. Of the adolescents who remained totally abstinent, 65 percent remained involved in AA/NA and aftercare for a full year following treatment. Only 11 percent who stayed abstinent did not participate in sobriety support groups.

According to Norman Hoffman of CATOR, 20 to 40 percent of treated adolescents are still sober one year following their discharge from inpatient treatment. Adolescents who stay involved in AA/NA *and* long-term outpatient therapy, and whose parents are involved in their treatment, have a much higher chance of staying sober than those who do not.

These are the elements that need to exist in programs if adolescents are to maintain lasting sobriety when they leave treatment. Parents must get involved and stay involved, and we must see to it that adolescents have long-term participation in both AA/NA *and* professional counseling. Without this, we are compromising adolescent recovery rates.

Chapter
3

Normal Adolescent Development

Chemically dependent adolescents and those who care about them need to understand the **normal adolescent developmental** process. The primary goal of this process is to develop the capacity for independent thought and independent action. This is how we become adults. Between the ages of thirteen and nineteen, adolescents need to complete four major tasks in learning to be independent. These tasks are (1) **individuation,** (2) **separation,** (3) **autonomy,** and (4) **cooperation.**

This is an unconscious process: adolescents are internally driven to complete these tasks. They repeat some of these tasks over and over again at different stages during the adolescent years. Let's look at each of these tasks because it's important to understand this internal drive to be independent.

1. *Individuation* means "I am separate from them; I am different. I am not just a chip off the old block. I have some unique things about me. I may look like my mother, but I am different from my mother. I am more than just my mom and dad's son or daughter. I am me; a separate and unique person."

Until the age of seventeen or eighteen most adolescents

have no sense of who they are. They share other people's identity through relationships and/or attachments. They are the son or daughter of...and a student at...[school]. They have no identity of their own. Adolescents struggle for a personal identity. It's an insult to constantly be referred to as "Don and Pauline's little boy, Jeff."

2. *Separation* means "I have to separate from my family. My parents have controlled my environment, my thoughts, and my access to the world for thirteen or fourteen years. If I'm to become an adult, I've got to break away from them and their influence. I have to stop seeing the world through their eyes and start seeing the world through my own eyes. And in order to do that, I need 'my own space.'"

Adolescents need to complete four major tasks in learning to be independent. These tasks are individuation, separation, autonomy, and cooperation.

How do adolescents separate? Well, this is the stage where they don't want to be seen in public with their parents. When they're at the mall, they will walk ten feet in front of Dad because they are embarrassed to be seen with him. The difficult issue here is that in order to become independent people they must experiment with roles and behavior that their parents don't always approve of or accept.

For instance, an adolescent girl may decide, "Today, I'm going to go out and walk around the mall and I'm going to act sophisticated all day, just like I'm rich, and like I know what this world's about. At lunch, I may order something like broccoli quiche." Now, if this adolescent's mom is close by, she's going to ask, "Since when do you eat *broccoli* and why are you standing like that? And what do you mean, acting like you're rich? You don't have ten dollars in the bank!"

Mom would be evaluating everything her daughter did and sharing with the world that this wasn't who she was at all. Adolescents need to break away from their parents' views of them and distance themselves from their parents' influence.

Becoming independent means thinking for yourself. Until adolescence, youngsters usually let their parents and teachers think for them. Thinking for yourself means learning through the law of consequences, on your own, what's in your best interest.

What do we call somebody who believes everything they are told? "Sucker." "Gullible." "Dummy." So when adolescents are told, "This is the way it is," they say, "*I* don't think so. That's not the way *I* see it at all."

Adolescents need to start to evaluate the world based on their own experience and to critically evaluate people, places, and situations to develop the ability to be independent thinkers. They need to stop taking adult wisdom for their own. That's what adolescence is about.

3. *Autonomy* means "I have the right to self-govern." This occurs when adolescents start to develop their own values. The adolescent begins to realize, "I have the right to decide what is right for me and wrong for me; what's good for me, what's bad for me; what I believe in, what I don't believe in. I have the right to decide my religion. Just because my parents are Catholic doesn't mean I want to be.

"They say that I have to be in at midnight! Well, I think that's ridiculous. I don't think smoking pot is bad. Their generation was into alcohol." Adolescents stop accepting everything their parents say just because they said it.

4. *Cooperation* means adolescents figure out that if they're going to make it in this society, they have to cooperate with other people. They come to understand that

"No man is an island." For example, the adolescent may decide, "I want my own car. That means I've got to come up with some money. Coming up with the money means I've got to get a job. And getting a job means I've got to get along with the boss."

Adolescents finally get to the point where they start to see the whole picture—that is, they do *if* they've been allowed to get through the first three steps. If they haven't been given enough space to go through **individuation, separation,** and **autonomy,** or if they were too numbed out with chemicals to go through them, they're going to continue to struggle with these tasks and to act out that struggle into their twenties or beyond.

The story of an adolescent girl I counseled for a time will help illustrate this. Her name was Sandy and she was a "P.K."—a preacher's kid. Sandy had been brought to me because her parents found some marijuana in her bedroom. It turned out that Sandy was not seriously involved with drugs at all. As a matter of fact, she'd only smoked marijuana a couple of times. She was in a pretty good crowd and really not into using drugs. But she had been experimenting with them, and I saw her for a short while.

I'd only seen Sandy a few times when all of a sudden she started into the **individuation** stage. I could tell this was happening to her because I could see it. At first, this fifteen-year-old girl came to my office dressed just as cute as she could be—by adult standards. She wore matching sweaters and blouses and skirts and looked real "preppie."

One day I went out into the waiting room of my office looking for Sandy and she wasn't there. There were other teenagers standing around, but I didn't see Sandy. Then a girl stood up who was totally "punked out," and it was Sandy. There was a night-and-day difference in her. She had cut off all her hair and spiked it on top. It stood about two inches high and was dyed pink.

She was wearing really heavy makeup and had pierced every possible place in her ear. Anywhere Sandy could put a hole in her ear and stick an earring in it, one was there, and both her earlobes were stretched and hanging down. She was dressed in black leather and was wearing all the bondage gear, the chains and everything. I really didn't recognize her until she stood up and started coming toward me. Even then, the only way I recognized her was by her eyes.

I knew that the worst thing I could do would be to over-react to her appearance. Sandy came into my office, sat down, and we went on with our session. About halfway through the session, she looked at me and asked, "Come on now, what do you think?"

I asked, "Do you mean about the way you're dressed?"

Sandy said, "Yeah."

So I asked her, "Well, what do **you** think about it? That's what's important."

"Well, I just love it," Sandy said. "I think it's cool! I think it's awesome! It's now!"

And all I said was, "It probably is."

Then Sandy asked, "But what do **you** think about me in it?"

I said, "Sandy, I think you're a very attractive girl and that you're attractive in anything you wear. Personally, I don't like that particular outfit, but it seems as if it's important to you. And who am I to judge it? If you like it, it's fine. Now let's go on with our session."

I refused to make an issue of this, but Sandy's mom and dad were going nuts! Remember, this adolescent is a "P.K."! I kept saying to them, "Don't make a big deal out of this. Sandy's a good kid and she's really not in any trouble. Let her get through this."

Well, shortly following individuation, as I was seeing Sandy, we were faced with **separation,** which meant, "I've got to have some space to figure out who I am." She needed to experiment with roles away from her parents.

Sandy's dad said that when they went to the mall **he** walked ten feet in front of her. He was afraid his parishioners would see them together and know that she was his daughter. Separation was not a problem. He did not want to be seen in public with *her.*

Sandy started into this behavior right after she went into counseling. She was a really fine young girl until she started seeing me, which made it look as if I had done something to her. But I was not the cause of this. It was time for her to go through these adolescent development tasks, and this was the way she was going about it.

The next step was the big challenge. When she went into the third stage of this process, **autonomy**, it was a *big* problem. Guess what Sandy decided and announced one evening at the dinner table? She said to her parents, "I am not going to church anymore. That place is full of hypocrites. And I'm not going to any more of those stupid little covered-dish dinners. And besides that, I don't believe in the Bible!"

Well, somebody might as well have taken a wrecking ball and knocked that house right off its foundation. Dad lost it! But listen to what else she told her father. Sandy said, "Dad, the Bible wasn't written by God. It wasn't even written by Jesus. It was written by men, and men make mistakes. For all you know, that thing you've been following to the letter all of your life was written incorrectly and ain't even the way it's supposed to be! And you've lived your whole life by it. What if you get to heaven and God says, 'There were mistakes in that book'?" That's what she said!

We may laugh, but if you were in her dad's shoes you'd find this difficult too. Right? Still, look at the high level of thinking that it took for Sandy to come up with that. That's not small stuff. It takes **higher cortical brain activity** to be able to analyze, redefine, and then integrate something that serious. Her ability to think this through was admirable.

Sandy's struggle for her autonomy went on for a while, and the family tension got worse. But they trusted me and they managed to keep enough distance from her to let her complete this. Then, guess what happened on her own? You see, if adolescents learn something on their own, they'll believe it.

Sandy decided that being independent meant she had to have money so she could buy her own clothes. Her mom and dad would not pay for **these** clothes. To buy her own clothes, her own car, and the other things she wanted meant she had to get a job.

Sandy went to one of the fast food chains and interviewed for a job, and she went all "punked out." The manager of the store just laughed at her. He said, "Sandy, you can't be serious. I'm sure you're a sweet kid, but I can't have somebody behind the counter that scares the people away. Frankly, children will be afraid of you."

Sandy came to see me and she was crushed. She asked, "What should I do?"

"About what?" Again, I was not going to give her my adult wisdom because she would have rejected it.

"Well, I don't know what to do about the fast food guy not liking the way I dress."

"What do you want to do about it?" I inquired.

Sandy said, "I want a job. I want my own car. I want..."

And I said, "Well, if you want to be independent, having your own money does help."

Sandy asked me again, "What should I do?"

"I don't know, Sandy," I said. "You tell me. What should you do?" I knew she was smart enough to figure this out.

After a few minutes, she said, "Well, you know what I think? Maybe I could, like, take all this off, and go to the job interview dressed normal, and just go to work dressed normal, and then I could dress like this on my off time."

I said to her, "Sandy, this is an important thing. Don't

45

compromise your values if they're really important to you. Don't let anybody tell you how to dress or how to behave if you don't agree with it. But you have to decide what's more important—dressing like this and not having any money, or compromising a little and having money and having other things you want. You have to choose whatever is more important to you."

Sandy went on another job interview dressed normally. She got the job, and over a period of weeks her "punk" look began to disappear. Her hairstyle went back to normal and her regular clothes and makeup came back. The only thing she kept were all the earrings. Soon she also came back into the family fold.

At the last stage of this process, about a year later, Sandy told her father she was going back to church on her own, of her own free will, because she chose this as her religion. Most adolescents do finally choose to adopt most of the values they learn in the home.

During their adolescence, teenagers are going to test things. They can't accept facts about life from their parents. They have to find out for themselves if the things adults tell them are real. And guess what? When parents take a good look at it, a lot of the stuff they bought and still believe was handed down to them by their parents. Some of it wouldn't pass testing in the real world. Some of it wouldn't test out if they really challenged it.

That's what "family of origin" issues are about. Some adults find out at the age of thirty, forty, or fifty that they've lived their lives based on mistaken beliefs. Their parents convinced them that the world was a certain way, and sometimes their parents were operating on unhealthy ideas. It's healthy to challenge our belief systems.

We cannot say to adolescents, "Sit down and listen to me. I *know,* so accept my wisdom." Why? Because we're telling those adolescents to abandon themselves. They need to learn to think for themselves. The fact that we are adults doesn't mean that we have all the answers—and adolescents know that. They learn in their adolescent years that adults don't have all the answers they need. They move from worshiping adults as small children to resenting them as adolescents. Finally they come to agree with some of the things they've been told based on their own experience. But there will be other things they've been told that they will never come to believe.

Teenagers are going to test things. . . . They have to find out for themselves if the things adults tell them are real.

Let's look at the adolescent physical, emotional, and mental development process in detail, using a bio/psycho-social/cognitive model, to see what normal adolescents can do or should be able to do at different ages. I have divided the normal adolescent developmental tasks into two age ranges: **ages thirteen to fifteen** and **ages sixteen to nineteen**.

We need to keep in mind that (1) adolescents deal with the four issues of **individuation, separation, autonomy,** and **cooperation** on different levels throughout this entire period, and (2) that this is **normal** adolescent development. This is not about youngsters with problems or those who are chemically dependent. These are the important things that are supposed to happen to all adolescents between the ages of thirteen and nineteen.

NORMAL ADOLESCENT DEVELOPMENT

AGES 13 - 15	AGES 16 - 19

Physical
(BIO)

Rapid Physical Development Hormone Increase	Physical Maturity Hormone Maturity

Emotional
(PSYCHO-SOCIAL)

Psycho-Sexual Stress Ego Ideals Self-Conscious	Psycho-Sexual Adjustment Self-Concept Intimacy

Mental
(COGNITIVE)

Concrete — Abstract Time = Measurement	Formal Operational Thought Time Perspective

Ages 13 - 15: Physical (BIO)

Rapid Physical Development. Between the ages of thirteen and fifteen adolescents go through rapid physical development, second only to that experienced in infancy. There is no other time when we go through as much physical change and growth as during our first few years of life.

These adolescents are growing taller. Their arms and legs are getting longer and their feet and hands are growing larger. This is uncomfortable for them, and as adults we often tend to forget how uncomfortable it was for us. It's not comfortable to put on a lot of weight at one time and gain a lot in height.

This is uncomfortable for several reasons. We need to mentally fit our bodies to be comfortable. We have to work with them long enough to know how big they are. Before adolescents start growing so fast, they know how far their arms reach. They know where the tips of their fingers end. But if they go to bed one night and their hands grow, they are going to have problems with them in the morning, because they haven't mentally adjusted to them.

Sometimes when thirteen- or fourteen-year-olds are sitting in the middle of the living room floor, they may trip or fall two or three times when they start to get up and walk across the room. This does not mean that they're on drugs or that anything else is "wrong" with them. More likely, it means that in the last few months their feet have grown and they haven't mentally adjusted to them yet. Until they do, these adolescents may literally fall over their own feet at times.

Adolescents will also grow so fast at times that they actually experience "growing pains." This can be very painful and scary because it is not obvious to them why they are hurting.

A fourteen-year-old girl lives next door to me. Last fall when she started to school she was shorter than I. Now, in the course of only one school year, she is taller than I am. And this is an adolescent I physically looked down on at the end of last summer.

This child has had such pain in her shins that she has lain in bed at night and cried. Her doctor has said there's nothing wrong with her, but that she's not imaginging the pain. She does hurt. Because she's growing so quickly, her bones are thin and fragile. This means that it would be dangerous for her to participate in track or any other strenuous activities.

Another unfortunate thing about physical development during adolescence is that the nose grows before the rest of the face does. Some adolescents get an adult nose while they still have a baby face. For adolescents who are really caught up in what they look like, this can be a hideous sight. It would be for an adult, wouldn't it? If over the next year your nose doubled in size and your face didn't, how would you feel about that?

Recently we visited some relatives we hadn't seen for a while, and one of them was a young nephew of mine. I went into the house, and here was this really cute adolescent, about fifteen, with this great big nose on his face! I could see it when I walked in the front door.

The whole time we talked to this boy, he turned his face away from us. I knew what he was doing. He was trying to hide his nose, and I don't blame him. But here's the thing: his father is a very attractive man. He's a large man with prominent facial bone structure. He has prominent jaws and a large nose, but it all fits. My nephew looks like his father and is growing into a build just like his dad's. But the nose came first and right now it doesn't look so good.

It's painful and it's hard not to be self-conscious with these kinds of things going on with the adolescent's body. Not to mention the other parts that are growing physically for the first time—genitals, for instance.

Just last summer, at twelve, Steve was able to take a running start out of his garage, run as fast as he could, jump on the back of his bike, and plow down that road like a streak of lightning. This summer he goes out, takes his running start and flies out there, jumps on his bike, and thinks he's killed himself. He doubles up and falls over. And as he's lying there on the ground in agony, with his eyes watering, he's wondering, "What's changed?"

Last year Paula ran across the backyard like a gazelle. This year things bounce. So Paula stops running because she doesn't know what to do about that. She suddenly stops doing something that's always been fun to do and made her feel good about herself. Now it makes her embarrassed.

Boys and girls experience the same thing. As preadolescents they didn't have the parts that they have now. They had them of course, but they were small and inconspicuous. Adolescents find they have things growing on them and they don't know what to do about it or how to adjust to them. Today you may be laughing at this, but inside, most thirteen- to fifteen-year-old adolescents don't find it very funny and they are very self-conscious about it. This stuff is brand-new to them. It's strange trying to adjust to a body that suddenly has sexual organs.

One group of special concern is the "early bloomers"— adolescents who at thirteen look seventeen. "Early bloomer" girls have fully developed breasts and hips and everything that goes with them. These girls walk with their shoulders hunched because they are embarrassed. In the sixth or seventh grade, they don't want anyone to be able to tell that they have breasts.

With "early bloomer" boys it's the same thing. They get really big and their muscles develop. These boys slouch so they won't stand out so much from the rest of the guys.

"Early bloomer" adolescents are under a great deal of pressure because they are expected to perform like seventeen- or eighteen-year-olds when they are much younger than that mentally and emotionally.

Being a "late bloomer" is also stressful. These are boys and girls who are smaller and are slower in developing sexually than other adolescents their age. These adolescents generally feel insecure and inadequate and typically they are treated as if they are younger, less capable, and more immature than they actually are by both authority figures and peers.

Hormone Increase. Adolescents also experience an increase in hormones at this age—big time. This is why all the dreams and fantasies start and where a growing interest in sexually oriented magazines and movies and in talking to friends about sex comes from. When adolescents experience this increase in hormones they start to have desires. All of a sudden they realize that when they get close to someone of the opposite sex they experience new body sensations. And they don't know how to handle this.

And guess what they discover? They find that society still has major "no-talk" rules about all of this. At this age, the thing adolescents are most preoccupied with is the sexual organs they're developing. They wonder whether or not the guy across the room has the same thing, and how all this stuff works. They have strong desires that they don't know how to cope with, and they are hard-pressed to find an authority figure with whom they can discuss these feelings.

Adolescents don't talk about this at home, at school, or in treatment centers. Why? Because their parents, teachers, and many trained professionals don't know what to do with it or how to talk about it. And do you know why these people don't know how to deal with this? Because nobody told them.

The following incident happened to me was when I was working with a boy about sixteen years old who had been sober for six months. Keep in mind that chemically dependent adolescents or adolescents with other serious problems are often delayed in their normal adolescent development. At sixteen, this boy was experiencing some of the things he should have been through at a much younger age.

David was in my adolescent sobriety group, and one day as our session was about to start, I asked the group members, "Does anybody need to talk about anything?" David raised his hand and he was red from the neck up. I knew it had to be bad because he was so red-faced; there's not much that adolescents are afraid to talk about in treatment. I was fairly new at this business and apprehensive, but I said, "All right, David, what is it?"

"Aw, nothing," he said. "Go on, we'll talk about it later." So we started into the group session and were into it about a half hour when David said, "Wait, I've got to talk about this."

"All right, what is it?" David's face was still red. He said, "Well, Tammy, I am so preoccupied with sex I can't think about anything else, and it's been like this for weeks. I go to bed thinking about it. I wake up thinking about it. I think about it all the way through school. I think about it all the time in group. *Everything* seems sexual to me!"

My reaction to this was, "Oh, no!" I did not know what to do. I thought perhaps it wasn't even *legal* to bring this subject up. This was at a time when there was controversy over whether we could teach sex education in the schools. I didn't know what was legal and what wasn't and I didn't know what to do.

Because I was a person who didn't know what to do and new to the field and scared, I said, "Can we talk about this alone after group?"

David said, "OK. But you don't realize, Tammy, that even opening the refrigerator door is a sexual experience!" By now, the whole group was on the floor laughing.

The "not so funny" part of this was that David was asking for somebody to help him deal with what was happening to him. Unfortunately, he had a counselor at the time who didn't know how to do it. I'm hoping that we've progressed past that point.

Age 13 - 15: Emotional (PSYCHO-SOCIAL)

Psycho-sexual Stress. Another disturbing thing, at least to most parents, is that between ages thirteen and fifteen adolescents have developed sexual capabilities. They don't always know exactly what to do with this new "equipment" but they are finding out. Typically, adolescents feel stressed, uncomfortable, scared, and confused about their new sexual development.

Ego Ideals. In the early teens, adolescents are also experiencing something called "ego ideals." At about the age of eleven or twelve they start to feel the need to get out from under Mom and Dad's control and to develop their own identity. They want to become independent but at this point they can't do it alone. Adolescents begin to rely heavily on their peer group during this time. They think, "I can take a step out and be semi-independent and still have my friends for support. These people are most like me and they have the same value system that I want to have."

This is the age when adolescents fall in love with rock stars, movie and TV personalities, and professional athletes—that is, if they're lucky. If they are not so lucky, they may find people or things to worship and idolize that are not so healthy. Michael Jackson is a lot better than some things they could choose. It's very important for them to have an idol that they can begin to role-model after and aspire to become like.

A young male adolescent will say, "Michael represents what's important to me, and I want to be just like him!" He will have posters of Michael Jackson up all over his room, and so will all his friends if that's who they want to be like. That's what having a peer group is all about.

Unfortunately, at this age adolescents are also most at risk to be attracted to various "cult" type activities. Between the ages of thirteen and fifteen is the ideal time for satanic groups, as well as some of the fanatical religious groups such as the "Moonies" and others like them, to get their hands on adolescents. Why? It is because of the adolescent's drive to complete the developmental tasks of *individuation, separation,* and *autonomy.*

In working through these tasks adolescents have some important needs including (1) to be listened to, (2) to be understood, (3) to be taken seriously, and (4) to be affirmed as people (Glenn, 1987). They need to have their ideas and opinions count and to feel that their participation is important.

Often, people recruiting for cults are able to make adolescents feel that, for the first time in their lives, somebody is listening to what they are thinking and saying. Unfortunately, what many of these groups stand for, believe in, or are trying to sell the adolescent is often very unhealthy. At times, it is even dangerous.

At this age, adolescents are able to recognize that there is a difference between listening and *really* listening. Adolescents know that they are not being listened to when they are talking to people who are busy thinking about something else. Isn't that how many adults listen to adolescents? We often focus on what we want them to hear from us, and on what we are going to say next, rather than listening to what adolescents are saying.

Being understood means that adolescents wish adults would try to stand in their shoes for a few minutes. They wish that adults would try to go back and remember when they were fifteen and what it would have been like for them to experience what the teenager is going through at this moment.

Adolescents want adults to *listen,* to try to *understand,* and to take them and what they are saying seriously. Instead, many adults act as if the adolescent's problems are ridiculous and unimportant. But to adolescents at this age, and in their stage in life, their concerns are *major* problems.

Adolescents need **role models** at this age. They need them and seek them out. Adolescents will imitate the behavior of anyone who has the things they want right now and the life-style that supports and matches up with the things they want. Quite often, this doesn't match up with what their parents want for them. Again, parents can't help but look at the "big picture" somewhere in the future, like college and a career for the adolescent, because that's important in the world adults live in every day. But at age thirteen to fifteen, those things are not yet important and the adolescents' "big picture" has in it what they want today.

For example, I had a typical middle-class adolescent in counseling with me who was chemically dependent. He was an athlete and I didn't have any place to put him. There was no program available at that time for him. So I decided to put him in with some chemically dependent boys from the state reform school program for adjudicated youth that I was running. Big mistake!

One adolescent in this group was a "biker" type. Tim had a motorcycle and he had money. He'd used drugs and dealt drugs, and he'd been through the whole scene of "street" experience. He was a big, muscular, good-looking young man who prided himself on being able to "beat the tar" out of anybody who had enough "guts" to challenge him. And he was "cool" in terms of what adolescents think are cool. He had the right "shades" and wore the right clothes. He was "Mr. Together."

Well, needless to say, my young chemically dependent athlete came into this group and identified strongly with Tim. Why? Because Tim was powerful, he had money, he was cool, and he had lots of girls; in fact, Tim had all the girls he wanted. At fifteen, most boys want girls; they will do whatever they believe they need to do to get their attention.

Because Tim had that , the obvious thing to do was to act like Tim. So this boy started imitating Tim, and he learned far more from Tim than he really ever needed to know. That boy never did return to the child he was before I placed him in that program, and I'm sure his parents didn't appreciate it. I know I wouldn't have.

Self-Conscious. Between ages thirteen and fifteen, adolescents are "self-conscious" rather than "other" conscious: *"Hello, how am I?" "How do I look?" "What can you do for me?" "What can I do you out of?" "Can you think of anything more important to you or to me than* **ME?"**

At this age they also don't know how to be intimate. Adolescents may change their "best friend" weekly because they do not have adequate bonding skills. They have not developed the ability or the skills to be able to relate to other people on an intimate level. They are still self-centered, and at this age that's normal.

To illustrate this, one day I was working with a room full of thirteen- to fifteen-year-olds in a therapy group. One of the group members, whom I will call Veronica, announced that right after group she was going to commit suicide. Veronica said her parents were gone, the car was at home, and she knew where the keys were. She said she was going to turn the car engine on, leave the garage door down, lie down to sleep in the front seat, and gas herself. It was a pretty traumatic thing for her to say and it was scary. Veronica had said she was going to kill herself, and she had the means and the ability to do it.

I looked around the group at the other adolescents, who were all under the age of fifteen. One girl was filing her nails; somebody bounced a spitwad off the ceiling; somebody else was picking his toes. Nobody was paying any attention. I looked around and was astonished that somebody could say, "I'm going to kill myself and I have all the means to do it," and nobody seemed to care.

So I kept looking around and then I asked the group, "Hey, group! Did you hear what Veronica just said?" I got their attention for a minute because I raised my voice. They all looked at each other, expressionless, and no one said anything. So I asked, "Does anybody *care* about what Veronica just said?" They all sat there for a minute until I said, *"Somebody* in this group say *something."* Then I sat back while they looked at each other for another couple of minutes. Now they were under pressure.

Finally, one adolescent said, "Hey, Veronica, don't do it, man." Then it was back to filing the nails and bouncing the spitballs.

I was upset by this because it was before I understood that there was a reason for their apathy. They hadn't yet developed their intimacy skills enough to be able to respond appropriately. They were still very self-centered and were just coming out of this stage. They didn't know what to say.

If adolescents don't know how to be intimate with someone, how do they know what they're supposed to say? If I tell them, "What you said to Veronica wasn't much help," they will ask, "Well, what should I have said?"

Adolescents may want to be helpful but don't know how to go about it. If they are expected to be intimate and to be solid, effective members of a support group at ages thirteen and fourteen, they will probably wind up doing a lot of play-acting.

These adolescents may want to be sincerely caring of others but it may not yet be possible for them, and that's OK. At this age, it doesn't mean that there is anything wrong with adolescents who mentally go in and out of themselves and their own thoughts. They can try, however, and learn through practice; but we can't expect them to be able to stay in heated interactions with others over long periods of time.

Adolescents can practice this by doing exercises which help them to understand that there is a place inside where they go and look at themselves. Then they get out of themselves and listen to somebody else. And that very well may be the best that they can do for now.

At this age, there are some kinds of emotions adolescents have that they can't identify. Even when they can identify them, often they can't label them. Adolescents learn what certain feelings mean by talking about them and comparing other adolescents' feelings with their own. They find out what makes those feelings happen in other adolescents and what they call them. For example, if adolescents report that their stomachs are churning and the muscles are tight in the backs of their necks, they are probably describing feelings that others have experienced too. They can then name these feelings and talk about them.

We can only expect adolescents to do the best they can. Sometimes they will be successful and other times they will not. This doesn't mean that they are "not trying," however. It means that they are still struggling with the development of intimacy skills. A thirteen- or fourteen-year-old can't be expected to be able to relate to others the way a sixteen- or nineteen-year-old can.

Age 13 - 15: Mental Development (COGNITIVE)

Concrete vs. Abstract Thinking. Up to the age of thirteen most children think in "concrete" terms meaning, "I've got to see it, taste it, touch it, and feel it to know about it." Before age thirteen, children can't really talk about "ideas" because they can't process them. They haven't yet developed the higher cortical regions of their brains. It's not that they are lazy or that they won't try. For them, if something isn't "concrete" it isn't there. Something has to be tangible in order for them to think or talk about it.

Watch an infant crawl across the floor after a cookie. If you throw a blanket over the cookie, the child will look away as if the cookie has disappeared rather than lift the blanket, knowing it's still there. The same principle applies to the adolescent. These youngsters aren't dumb. They just haven't developed that far yet mentally. When people start to talk about abstract principles to adolescents who can still think only in concrete terms, they just "nod out." Their brains can't process the information.

When adolescents get to be about twelve or thirteen they start to develop the ability to think abstractly. Now they can begin to think about things that aren't there. They still can't get into thinking through complex issues but they are beginning to do some of this. That's why we generally don't teach algebra until the eighth and ninth grades. Until then, most adolescents' brains haven't developed to the point that they can process abstract concepts. And some youngsters may struggle even then because this skill is so new to them.

If adolescents get lost easily in a counseling or education program, it means that the counselors or teachers should gear that program down to them. If the material that helpers are trying to teach is beyond adolescent comprehension, they are wasting everyone's time. The adolescents won't "get it," and it won't be their fault.

AA/NA, by the way, are not concrete programs. They are abstract programs, which means that young adolescents often hate them—and that makes sense. A twelve- to fourteen-year-old can't understand what "Turn It Over" or what the Twelve Steps mean. "Powerlessness": what's that?

Adolescents don't have to hate AA/NA. They will, however, if these programs are over their heads and no one takes the time to help them understand what's going on. When adolescents attempt to follow someone who is talking over their heads, they may try for a while and then give up mentally.

When adolescents go to meetings they are anxious at first. When they try to understand and then don't "get it," they start getting bored. A solution I've found to this is to assign temporary thirty-day sponsors for adolescents. I recruit people from Twelve-Step programs who have a desire to work with young people and who will commit to working with an adolescent for thirty days. They don't have to see these teenagers every day for thirty days but should become very involved as sponsors in talking to them and explaining what is going on.

It is important to teach these volunteers what being an adolescent means. I tell them, "I know that you have sponsored twenty-five people before, Joe, but this one is fourteen."

It's also important that these sponsors introduce adolescents to folks who will respond to them and take them to the "better" meetings. (Most communities have "good" meetings and "better" meetings.) If the first experiences the adolescents have with AA/NA are unpleasant ones, it will be difficult to convince them that it won't be the same at every meeting.

If young persons have been using drugs since they were ten or eleven and haven't worked through some of the normal adolescent tasks, they may still be very self-conscious. They may believe that "Everybody is staring at me" or "Nobody here likes me!" If adolescents feel that way from the start, it will be hard for them to believe they are welcome and accepted and that they can find support there.

Adolescents need to be put in touch with a temporary sponsor who will stay with them for a while after a meeting and say "Look, when they were talking about the First Step, let me tell you what that means to me." Adolescent newcomers are not going to understand many of the words and the concepts that they hear. They need someone who won't try to explain the whole AA program to them all at once—just one Step at a time, one day at a time.

Time-Measurement. Adolescents under the age of fifteen do not yet have a conceptual understanding of time. Very young children have no concept of time whatever. Isn't that what drives us crazy about having little ones in the house? They stand there saying, "Now! Now! I have to go to the bathroom *now!*" Not two minutes from now. Not when you have finished talking on the phone, but *now.*

When I tell my five-year-old nephew, Brian, "Honey, you can have those sweet pickles after dinner," he hits the floor and starts crying. To him, when I say "after dinner" I may as well say "when you are sixteen." At age fourteen, adolescents are not a great deal past this stage of development regarding time, and that's normal. They may have memorized some rituals and habits, but mentally they are not a great deal past that.

As children get older they begin to see time as a measurement, as pieces of a day or a year, but that's all it is. Adolescents under the age of fifteen or sixteen get through life knowing that there are sixty minutes in an hour and twenty-four hours in a day because they have memorized this; however, they have no real understanding of it, nor should they be expected to at this age.

Because adolescents don't have any perspective of time at age thirteen to fifteen, it is hard for them to wait for things to happen. When adolescents say "now," it's the end of the world when something they want to happen doesn't happen right then. They may be told that they "lack impulse control" as if it's a fault they have, but that's the way it's supposed to be. For their age, that's normal.

They can learn to develop the ability to wait, but it's not going to happen all at once or just because someone tells them to do it. To them "tomorrow" or "next week" might as well be six years from now, because it means the same thing in their minds. It's all the same; it's all "not now." These adolescents will say, "Forget that! I want this now! I'm not waiting!" Then they will focus all their attention on getting to do or have whatever it is they want.

Waiting for a driver's license can seem like forever to an adolescent. When we tell adolescents at age fourteen that in two years they'll be able to drive, we may as well say, "when you are forty." At this age, a school year seems like an eternity! Until adolescents have this perspective on time, they cannot delay gratification, which simply means waiting for what they want.

This tends to end for adolescents about the time they get their driver's license. Once that big wait is over for them, the rest of life picks up speed. Prior to that time, a moment lasts an hour.

Age 16 - 19: Physical (BIO)

Physical Maturity. Between ages sixteen and nineteen, adolescents reach physical maturity. They have adjusted to their physically mature bodies and walk erect because they are proud of what they have. It is difficult to figure out who were the early bloomers or the late bloomers. Now just walk into any high school and watch all of them strutting their stuff.

Both girls and boys find the smallest bikinis they can to wear to the beach. Their parents are shocked with the change in them. Adolescents who wouldn't come out of the bedroom or the bathroom between ages thirteen to fifteen now want to run around the house naked. They want to let the whole world see how beautiful their bodies are. And they should enjoy them because most of us just don't feel that way about our bodies very long, do we?

Age 16 - 19: Emotional (PSYCHO-SOCIAL)

Psycho-sexual Adjustment. By age sixteen to nineteen most adolescents have adjusted emotionally to their sexual capabilities. They are comfortable with their bodies by now, even if not completely satisfied. They know what sex is about and most of them are experimenting with it or exploring possible opportunities.

Self-concept. Between ages sixteen to nineteen adolescents move from being self-conscious—or focusing on how they look and seem to be to others—to developing self-concept. They begin the process of trying to define who they are, what they value, and what is important to them. Who am I? What am I about? What do I believe in? What's right and wrong? What religion do I want to be? What can I do? What am I good at? What are my strengths and weaknesses?

Intimacy. At this age, intimacy becomes a very important issue, both with the opposite sex and the same sex. Adolescents develop skills in communicating on a deep level with someone else. Usually they have a "best friend," one person with whom they share themselves more than with anybody else in the whole world. They feel destroyed when they "break up" with a steady boy friend or girl friend or when they get into a fight with their best friend.

Adolescents make their first attempts at intimacy blindly. They don't realize yet that things happen in relationships: things go wrong, people fight, and betrayals happen consciously and unconsciously. Adolescents will share everything with their closest friend. They are devastated when that person does anything to them that hurts, because they invested everything. Sometimes they can't believe what the other person has done to them! "I told her my deepest secrets, and she told Suzie!"

At age sixteen to nineteen, breaking up with a steady girl friend or boyfriend is usually the most serious thing adolescents have ever coped with. It is as traumatic for them as it is for adults who go home one night to hear their spouse announce, "I'm leaving you! I'm out of here!"

Adolescents do not feel as if they are being taken seriously when parents say, "Oh, honey, there's a million other girls like her [or boys like him] out there. You'll find another one. You'll be in love with somebody else next week." What adolescents hear is their parents saying, "Your pain is no big deal, and you don't count." They want to scream, "You're not listening! Don't you hear me? I'm telling you that I *love* this person and she's dating somebody else!"

Adolescents want *affirmation* as persons. They want parents to say, "I hear what you're saying. This must really hurt you because you are real. I've experienced that too. This must be very painful for you!" Adolescents want their parents to validate the things they say to them as being significant and as having some real meaning. Even those adolescents with behavioral problems will respond to people who relate to them in this way.

Age 16 - 19: Mental Development (COGNITIVE)

Formal Operational Thought. By the age of sixteen to nineteen adolescents develop the ability to do what Piaget called "formal operational thinking." This is the highest form of thinking in which we can engage. Complex ideas and concepts, cause and effect relationships, hypothesis and deductions all come from our ability to complete formal operational thinking.

As a simple example of formal operational thought, one day an adolescent said to me, "You know what? Today, I was just sitting there in school, and I was thinking about my future. And then I started thinking, 'Why am I thinking about my future?' Then I started thinking, 'Why am I thinking about why I'm thinking about my future?'" That's formal operational thinking going on.

This is where adolescents can really get into "space cadet" kinds of thinking and can also get really creative. People may make fun of them when they do this, because when they've just found this new capacity they tend to experiment with it extensively. Adolescents have to practice in order to think on this level.

Time Perspective. When adolescents are about sixteen, all of a sudden they develop the ability to understand time and how things move through time. They come to understand their place in time—that they have a past that was this many years ago, that they are in the present now, and that they really will be forty someday.

The Adolescent Development Process and Preventing Adolescent Relapse

Understanding the adolescent development process is

important in preventing adolescent relapse because most chemically dependent adolescents are two to four years behind in their normal development process. The fact that they went to treatment and now have six months or a year free of alcohol and drugs doesn't mean that they are going to think, feel, and act like nonaddicted adolescents of the same age. This makes working a recovery program hard for them and adds to their risk of relapse.

To be a recovering chemically dependent adolescent in our society is extremely stressful and poses many problems.

To be a recovering chemically dependent adolescent in society is extremely stressful and poses many problems. The primary problem is that these youngsters have difficulty finding a place where they fit in. They can interact with recovering chemically dependent adults in terms of working on their recovery, but they do not exactly fit socially. Adults tend to stay in an authoritarian role, and these children need a peer group to rely on in order to complete their adolescent developmental tasks.

Recovering adolescents need space to achieve separation and autonomy. They require the consistency of a peer support group in order to find out who they are and to exert their own independence. This can present a problem in communities that lack sobriety-focused adolescents. In many parts of the country, particularly outside of large cities, we don't have many recovering adolescents in Twelve-Step groups. Some adolescents don't know very many (and sometimes not even one) other recovering chemically dependent adolescent with whom they can socialize and bond, and these adolescents are left "in limbo."

Recovering chemically dependent adolescents do not interact well with peers who are not chemically dependent until they are further along in their recovery process. Non-chemically dependent adolescents can feel uncomfortable around those who are, because recovering adolescents often appear more harsh and less capable. Often they haven't graduated cognitively to the same level as adolescents of their age who aren't chemically dependent.

This is complicated by the fact that they are usually "street wise." These conflicting issues confuse and frighten non-recovering adolescents, causing recovering adolescents to remain at risk because they can't find peer groups with which to identify. If we don't find strong recovering groups of young people to provide support for very young or newly recovering adolescents, it will continue to be difficult to keep them in Twelve-Step programs.

Adolescents who come from seriously dysfunctional families, who have psychiatric problems, or who are chemically dependent typically have delayed development. Adolescents who are chemically dependent and those people who are around them need to understand this. Otherwise, neither the adolescent nor those who are trying to help them will understand why chemically dependent adolescents act differently in many ways from normal adolescents even after they get "clean and sober."

It is not when adolescents first start using chemicals that their normal development stops. It is not when they had their first experimental taste of beer at age eight, ten, twelve, or fourteen. It is not the first time they smoked a joint or the first couple of times that they got drunk that their development stopped. It was when they started bonding emotionally to the chemical.

Normal development stops when adolescents start using chemicals to help them accomplish something or to "make it" on the path that lies before them. It is when they start to use chemicals to deal with normal adolescent development tasks, family problems, school problems, asking a girl out, or with going out with that guy. It is when the adolescent develops a pathological or dependent relationship with a drug that development stops.

Most chemically dependent adolescents do not act, think, or feel in the ways I have described as normal until they are well along in their recovery process. They may not be acting their age in regard to their behavior, in managing their feelings and emotions, in relating to others, or in processing information mentally.

We learn from experiencing the consequences of our behavior. Chemical use prevents or changes these experiences. Information altered by chemical use or learning done while under the influence doesn't usually match very well with reality when chemically dependent adolescents become sober. Their use of chemicals during the years when adolescent development would have normally taken place leaves them developmentally immature for their age and size. There is usually much that they need to learn for the first time or to learn over again in sobriety.

In preventing adolescent relapse, we have to look at four issues based on the normal adolescent model.

1. We have to find resources such as young people's AA or ongoing sobriety groups and sober social activities which are held on a regular basis, and make them available to recovering chemically dependent adolescents.

2. We have to look at their orientation to Twelve-Step programs. It is very important that recovering adolescents get into a Twelve-Step support group. However, the method by which most of them are introduced to it at present often fails to get them to bond with other recovering people. Generally,

we don't take enough time at first to teach them what these programs are about.

I believe it is a mistake to force adolescents into AA before they understand the reasons for going to Twelve-Step meetings and how they can benefit from them. We need to introduce them to recovering people who attend those meetings before we send them and get them matched up with temporary sponsors before beginning their Twelve-Step work.

Most chemically dependent adolescents do not act, think, or feel in the ways I have described as normal until they are well along in their recovery process.

---

3. We have to recognize their cognitive limitations, particularly around lack of impulse control. When chemically dependent adolescents cannot control impulses, they are at major risk for relapse. We have to help them to develop a time perspective by teaching them how to wait their turn and how long a minute is, and to recognize that their inability to think first and delay gratification will set them up for relapse.

4. Recovering chemically dependent adolescents need opportunities to practice learning from the consequences of their behavior how to cooperate with others and how to live comfortably without drugs in the real world.

For example, one sixteen-year-old adolescent I saw in therapy was large in size for his age, but due to his drug use he had not developed mentally the way he should have. Jeff had a major impulse control problem, meaning he couldn't wait for anything he wanted. He couldn't delay gratification to save his life. We knew that when we got him chemically free he could catch up, but it would take some effort.

I make it a practice to have adolescents share their problems and recovery goals with their group. Except for their really sensitive issues such as incest or rape, everything that adolescents need to work on should be known by their group.

Everyone in Jeff's group knew that he had impulse control problems. They knew that Jeff couldn't delay gratification because he did not have the time perspective that he should have developed by age sixteen because of his chemical use. They knew that one of his recovery goals was to bring himself up to a sixteen- or seventeen-year-old level in this area. In working on this we structured situations where he had to wait for things he wanted and take his turn.

One day I had an opportunity to see Jeff's group in action, helping him with this problem. I was not scheduled to be around at the time, and no one in the group was aware that I was in the hall where the adolescents were lining up for dinner. All of a sudden I heard Kevin, who was the same age as Jeff but half his size, say, "Hey, Jeff, what are you doing?" The rest of the adolescents in Jeff's group were standing there with their arms folded, glaring at Jeff and tapping their feet.

"Look, Jeff," Kevin went on, "you are trying to crowd in front of everyone in this line. This is one of your problems, Jeff. Now, why don't you just go to the back of the line and practice waiting your turn just like the rest of us?" And everyone from Jeff's group was nodding in agreement and saying, "Yeah!"

Now big Jeff might have been able to take them all on, but he didn't want to because this was his group and he respected them. So he went to the back of the line and accepted the fact that he had to wait. Jeff learned far more from what Kevin and the other adolescents said to him that day than if I had said it. It is this kind of peer support and these kinds of experiences that chemically dependent adolescents need to have to catch up with normal adolescents their age.

Emotionally and mentally, chemically dependent adolescents can almost always catch up in their adolescent developmental process, but it takes effort, patience, time, and staying drug free. And of these, the most important is staying drug free.

Chapter

4

Common Adolescent Disorders

Don, a fifteen-year-old chemically dependent adolescent, was sent to our agency by the juvenile state school system to be evaluated for treatment. Don came with a long history. He had been for the last six months in a reform school for boys — this was his third incarceration — and he had been seen by numerous psychiatrists and social workers since early childhood. Due to lack of financial resources that would allow Don to participate in a more structured inpatient program, he was involved in this program for three months and, in many respects, appeared to be making great strides. Don was cooperative in treatment and posed no major problem. He considered himself to be chemically dependent and talked about himself in this way. He was very active in AA and NA meetings in our community, and he had a sponsor.

Around three months into the program, however, the staff found out that Don was still actively using chemicals as well as involved in drug dealing and breaking and entering activities. The treatment staff was very frustrated because they believed that Don had been making great improvement. They felt tricked and betrayed when they found out that he had been misleading them. What had gone wrong with Don's treatment?

Don was clearly chemically dependent, in the midst of a full-blown addiction. He had begun using chemicals regularly at about age ten. After he had been released from our program and sent back to the reform school system, the staff became aware of numerous other things about Don. They learned that he had been seriously physically and sexually abused as a small child by his mother, and he had been living in a foster care situation since the age of eight. He did not know who or where his father was and he had not seen his mother since he was eight or nine years old.

Don obviously had a conduct disorder in that he was unable to manage his behavior. As a result of his inability to manage his behavior, Don had also developed a strong criminal thinking element from older siblings as well as multiple incarcerations in reform schools. He admitted to enjoying the excitement of running the streets at night, being involved in criminal activities, and being pursued by the police department. This was why Don didn't respond to treatment and why he found it necessary to fool everyone. Don also suffered from post traumatic stress disorder (PTSD) as a result of being physically and sexually abused as a child.

Don is representative of the many adolescents who are more than chemically dependent, those we call "dual or multiple diagnosed." In addition to being chemically dependent, he also had two other significant problems: conduct disorder and PTSD.

Coping with dual diagnosis in adolescence is a requirement in a chemical dependency treatment program. There are some professionals in this field who believe that all chemically dependent adolescents are dually diagnosed, but I don't agree. I have treated numerous adolescents who were chemically dependent and had no other accompanying disorders. However, a large number of chemically dependent adolescents do have other disorders which make them dual or multiple diagnosed and place them at high risk of relapse. It is therefore critical that all chemical dependency programs be able to treat dual diagnosis.

A large number of chemically dependent adolescents do have other disorders.... It is critical that all chemical dependency programs be able to treat dual diagnosis.

It is not possible to examine the entire list of disorders that can accompany chemical dependency in this book. Instead I will briefly review the six dual or multiple diagnosis disorders that we see most commonly in chemically dependent adolescents. These six disorders are (1) depression, (2) learning disabilities, (3) conduct disorder, (4) post traumatic stress disorder, (5) eating disorders, and (6) codependence. Let us take a closer look at the signs and symptoms of these disorders. If two or more of these symptoms are chronically present in your adolescent, you should arrange for an evaluation by a trained professional (psychiatrist, psychologist, or social worker) who has a background in chemical dependency as well as mental health.

Depression

Depression is seen in nearly 70 percent of the adolescents present at an adolescent chemical dependency treatment program. With depression comes serious threat through suicide ideation, or thinking about killing oneself and of ways to do it, or actual past suicide attempts. To help in recognizing depression, here are some common symptoms.

==

Symptoms of Depression

The symptoms of depression in adolescents include the following:

1. *a depressed mood, or irritable, most of the time;*
2. *a loss of interest or pleasure in most activities, including ones the adolescent was very involved with in the past;*
3. *a significant gain or loss of weight;*
4. *a marked increase or decrease in appetite;*
5. *either an inability to go to sleep (insomnia) or an inability to stay awake (hypersomnia);*
6. *chronic fatigue;*
7. *problems with memory;*
8. *feelings and expressions of worthlessness;*
9. *problems thinking or concentrating;*
10. *difficulty making decisions;*
11. *persistent thoughts of death or suicide.*

==

Depressed adolescents often spend a great deal of time in their rooms, showing little interest in socializing or in activities with friends. Depression, however, is a common symptom when an adolescent is going through detoxification and in the early recovery process. Very often it results from grief issues around giving up chemical use. This depression should gradually lift during treatment. Adolescents who do not recover from this depression prior to leaving an inpatient treatment program should have an evaluation by a psychologist or psychiatrist who has a background in chemical dependency. These adolescents may have a clinical depression that will not lift in recovery without professional help.

Some clues that will help you determine if depression is a dual diagnosis include (1) if the adolescent has experienced episodes of depression as a child or during adolescence, and (2) if these time periods in which the adolescent obviously had problems with depression occurred prior to drug use, or (3) if there are relatives who suffer from depression.

Learning Disabilities (LD)

According to the CATOR statistics, at least 17 to 24 percent of chemically dependent adolescents can be diagnosedd as learning disabled (LD) or at least require special education. These adolescents have usually progressed through school, but this disturbance has interfered with their ability to function or to progress normally in school.

==

Symptoms of LD

The adolescent with LD shows difficulty competing with peers in the same age-group with regard to
1. *reading comprehension,*
2. *spelling,*
3. *writing,*
4. *doing arithmetic or understanding arithmetic, and/or*
5. *understanding language or formulating language in conversation in spite of having normal, average, or above average IQs.*

It often affects their daily functioning within society, in such ways as having difficulty in figur-

ing out how much change to get back from cash
purchases, reading an employment application,
and following verbal or written instructions.
   The key to recognizing LD disturbances is that
they are not due to visual or hearing defects,
neurological disorders, or mental retardation.

==

The significance of LD and special education adolescents
is that they are behind in school. These adolescents will have
limited futures if they do not catch up to an average educational level so that they can function comfortably in our society. LD also contributes to very low self-esteem in adolescents and frustration in performing tasks expected of
them.

A second issue is the inability of LD adolescents to process
vital treatment information. To be effective, chemical dependency treatment requires that adolescents understand what
chemical dependency is and be able to process this understanding internally. Adolescents must know what being
chemically dependent means and be able to describe their
disease in their own words. Then they must become able to
self-apply that information. This means that they can describe the progression of symptoms of their own chemical
dependency and give examples of how this progression
played itself out in their lives. Finally, they have to learn to
accept their chemical dependency as a disease, which means
resolving their guilt, shame, and remorse about being chemically dependent.

These are the three primary objectives of an adolescent
chemical dependency treatment program; therefore, an adolescent's ability to understand and process this information is
vital. The methods used to assist adolescents in accom-

plishing these objectives are educational lectures, group therapy, and Twelve-Step program involvement in AA/NA.

Adolescents who have limited reading and comprehension skills will have to struggle to absorb and integrate the information they must have to stay sober. They will find staying sober to be extremely difficult due to their inability to figure out what is going on or to intellectually relate information about chemical dependency to their own experience.

Adolescents who are LD need to be evaluated by professionals who can clearly outline their learning limitations and provide treatment plans to help them catch up to other adolescents of their same age. When adolescents who are LD remain untreated they are at high risk for relapse. They will find it difficult to understand recovery or to enter the recovery process because they will not be able to comprehend or apply the information and guidance available to them in Twelve-Step meetings.

Conduct Disorders
This disorder appears in both males and females but appears to be in a much higher ratio in males.

===

Symptoms of Conduct Disorder
The symptoms of conduct disorders in adolescents include the following:
1. *stealing,*
2. *running away from home,*
3. *chronic lying,*
4. *truancy from school,*
5. *breaking into someone else's house, car, or business,*

6. *deliberately destroying other people's property,*
7. *being physically cruel to animals,*
8. *having forced others into sexual activity,*
9. *having used a weapon in a fight,*
10. *often initiating fights, and/or*
11. *being physically cruel to people.*

===

Conduct-disordered adolescents are in trouble, as illustrated by my story of Don at the beginning of this chapter. They cannot control their behavior. If these adolescents don't get into a treatment system where they have an opportunity to get control of their behavior through therapy, they are headed for major life problems and often prison. Many of these adolescents come from homes where someone else in the family is conduct disordered.

Conduct-disordered adolescents who come through the system are some of the toughest to treat. High success rates with these patients are often not realistic. We cannot expect to undo the things that these adolescents have already been through in the last fourteen or fifteen years of their lives. Many of them have suffered abuse or have been raised in a criminal environment. We can, however, make a difference with most of them and help them to change.

Most often these adolescents have not had a normal childhood or a functional family system. Usually they have been labeled in the schools and by their neighbors as "bad" adolescents and have been in and out of reform schools. I believe that adolescents learn what they live and that it is possible to convince adolescents that they are "bad" or "stupid." You may say, "these kids don't trust me." Why should they? Nobody else who qualifies as an adult has ever earned their trust. Many of them have experienced abuse by adults all their lives. Usually the "harder" these adolescents are, the worse abuse they have been through. These defenses that we see them put up are "self-preservation" techniques for them. If we had experienced what some of them have lived through, we would probably respond in the same ways.

If [conduct-disordered] adolescents don't get into a treatment system where they have an opportunity to get control of their behavior through therapy, they are headed for major life problems.

However, decisions have to be made regarding conduct-disordered adolescents in treatment. Mildly conduct-disordered adolescents can be integrated into traditional treatment programs and often respond very well. The more severely conduct-disordered adolescents, those who have been involved in heavy felonious crimes or who are extremely manipulative, violent, or criminal in their thoughts and their behaviors, may not be appropriate for all adolescent chemical dependency treatment programs. Sometimes these adolescents require specialized programs that can provide a great deal more structure and enforcement.

Post Traumatic Stress Disorder (PTSD)

It is not just Vietnam veterans who suffer from PTSD. Many chemically dependent adolescents who have experienced sexual, physical, or emotional abuse or who grew up in a "family war zone" also suffer PTSD. At least 40 percent of all chemically dependent adolescents have suffered physical, emotional, or sexual abuse as children. These adolescents have been victims of violent incidences such as rape, incest, physical and verbal battering, and these issues cannot be ignored in treatment. When adolescents are suffering from PTSD, they may act out, be uncontrollable, or be unable to respond to treatment for chemical dependency unless their PTSD is addressed also.

===

Symptoms of PTSD

PTSD may be present in adolescents who

1. experience recurrent and intrusive distressing dreams;

2. suddenly have a feeling that the traumatic event is reoccurring and that they are reliving the experiences;

3. have inappropriately intense emotional responses;

4. try to avoid certain people, places, and situations by "numbing off" or becoming totally unresponsive;

5. have difficulty recalling important aspects of their childhood, and sometimes have no memory or very little memory of their childhood at all;

6. have diminished interest in significant and important activities;

7. act out feelings of being isolated or estranged from others;

8. have a limited emotional range and are often unable to have loving feelings;

9. express a sense of a foreshortened future, meaning that they just don't see themselves as having any future: they don't believe that they are

*going to get married someday or that they will
even get any older;*

10. have problems sleeping;

11. have sudden outbursts of anger;

12. demonstrate difficulty in concentrating;

*13. sit in a room with their backs to the door,
keeping their eyes on everybody else and watch-
ing everything that is going on;*

*14. have a short attention span, which results
from having to be aware of all the other stimuli in
their surroundings;*

15. overreact to sudden or loud noises; or

*16. seem always to be on the defensive, ready to
fight and to protect themselves.*

===

In Vietnam veterans this hypervigilance is recognized as a
form of self-protection which people develop when they are
required to constantly "scope out" everything to make sure
that there isn't any danger. PTSD results when someone
fears for his or her life or personal integrity. Often, Vietnam
and other war veterans have been through weeks, months, a
year or more in a survival mode—and so have children who
have lived with abuse.

If someone came into your room late at night when you
were three or four years old and did things to you that you
find difficult even to think about as an adult, you were in a
survival mode as much as a soldier sitting in the jungle with a
machine gun in his hand. For that child the whole world was
a terrifying place, just as it was for the soldier: it was
catastrophic. By the time such children reach the age of fourteen, fifteen, or sixteen, they know that what happened to
them was not right.

When they were very young, these children may have figured that everybody was living like that, but instinctively they did not like it. Sexual abuse violates something in the spirit of children. It totally alters the way they look through those young eyes and see the world. When abuse is suspected because of obvious PTSD symptoms, an evaluation of physical, sexual, and emotional abuse needs to be done or, in other words, an investigation. If an adolescent is living in a situation where the active physical, sexual, or emotional abuse is presently occurring, intervention on the family must be made. The child may need to leave that home to be protected.

Adolescents who experience PTSD will not respond to treatment if we do not teach them how to identify the thoughts and feelings they are having. They need to recognize how their feelings about being abused affect the behavior they have now and learn to deal with these feelings without using chemicals.

These adolescents must acknowledge the pain that they suffered as children, process their feelings associated with the trauma they experienced, and recognize how symptoms of PTSD may be interfering with their ability to work a recovery program and to feel good about themselves.

PTSD adolescents can be difficult in treatment because they are often very hard to get close to. Very often, any authority figure represents to them someone who is in a power position to take advantage of them. These adolescents tend to isolate and try very hard not to bond either with adults or other adolescents.

Eating Disorders

Eating disorders are experienced by at least 11 percent of the chemically dependent adolescent population. Eating disorders include three specific disorders: (1) anorexia nervosa, (2) bulimia nervosa, and (3) compulsive overeating.

==

Symptoms of anorexia nervosa may be present in adolescents who

1. experience a major weight loss or fail to achieve a normal weight through their deliberate efforts to control their weight, using such methods as fasting, physical exercise, and appetite suppressants;

2. experience intense fear of gaining weight or becoming fat;

3. are overly preoccupied with being fat or with fat people;

4. have a disturbance in their body image. They may be 15 to 20 percent below normal weight and yet feel fat even though they obviously look very skinny or emaciated;

5. may talk about one part of the body being too fat; or

6. in females, starve themselves or exercise to the point of missing their menstrual cycles.

==

1. *Anorexia nervosa.* Anorexia is the least prevalent of the three major eating disorders, but it is a very serious condition. Some adolescents die from starving themselves. Anorexia is primarily experienced by adolescent girls. Although there are also males with anorexia, we see it far more frequently in the female population.

One anorectic adolescent with whom I worked named Pauline not only starved herself but had other compulsive behaviors related to managing her weight. She exercised very strenuously every day and was constantly reading magazines and books on weight management and how to stay thin and fit. Pauline was totally preoccupied with how she looked and was completely convinced that she was fat even though she was about five-feet, four-inches tall and weighed about ninety-five pounds.

Pauline existed on starvation diets. She would go as much as ten days without eating any food, just taking fluids. She also had difficulty eating when she did eat. She would pick at her food or move it around on the plate.

2. *Bulimia nervosa.* Bulimia is marked by recurrent episodes of binge eating during which the adolescent eats large quantities of food. After these adolescents lose control over their eating, they engage in methods for eliminating the calories they consumed during binging. They do this through self-induced vomiting following binges, the use of laxatives and diuretics (water pills), fasting, and vigorous exercise to prevent weight gain. Often, these adolescents begin to use amphetamines or over-the-counter appetite suppressants to manage their weight.

Another clue for this disorder is severely discolored or eroded front teeth. This symptom results from the action of the hydrochloric acid that is regurgitated from the stomach on tooth enamel. Like anorectic adolescents, bulimic adolescents are also over-concerned with their body shape and weight. They too have a total preoccupation, first with eating and then with getting rid of the food. Sometimes bulimic adolescents will not eat for a week and then their metabolism really starts to slow down. They starve themselves to the point of total obsession with food, and then they will consume a whole pizza, half a cake, and/or a whole pan of brownies. Then, to avoid gaining weight as a result of their binging, they will induce vomiting, purge their system with laxatives or over-exercise. This starve-binge-purge cycle is extremely stressful on the heart and other major organs.

One bulimic girl with whom I worked exercised for two hours every day. She would also go on what she called "vinegar and grapefruit" diets in which she ate only grapefruit, drank only water, and insisted on having vinegar with each of these "meals."

3. *Compulsive Overeating.* Yes, it is a disorder and, no, it doesn't get better by wishing it away. Dieting will not get rid of this disorder either. I believe that the best and most effective treatment for compulsive overeating is Overeaters Anonymous (OA) which uses a lifetime disease concept model and a Twelve-Step approach to recovery that has been very successful in helping people with this problem.

Compulsive overeating involves the consumption of large quantities of food in a short period of time, and it includes occasions such as Thanksgiving, Christmas, Easter, every Saturday or Tuesday night, or when we go out to eat. With compulsive overeating there is also a mental preoccupation with food, as with the other eating disorders. For example, while you were eating lunch today, you may have been thinking about what you were going to have for dinner later.

==

Symptoms of Compulsive Overeating

1. Feelings of being fat and persistent thoughts about being fat;

2. Buying clothes or dressing in ways which hide the body;

3. Weight fluctuations of more than ten pounds due to dieting and overeating;

4. Hiding the way one eats by eating alone in the car, the bedroom, or the bathroom;

5. Hoarding favorite foods;

6. Repeated attempts to control weight;

7. Health complications such as high blood pressure and heart disease resulting from eating habits; and

8. Guilt feelings associated with eating and thoughts such as "I should not be eating. I'm too fat. I should stop." These are the same thoughts and guilt feelings that alcoholics have when they are drinking and the same kind of mental preoccupation they have with alcohol.

===

Skip, a fifteen-year-old boy who had been quite involved with amphetamines throughout his chemical use, had not discussed his weight with me or mentioned any problems with his weight prior to entering treatment. Skip was sent to a twenty-eight-day inpatient treatment program and gained fifteen pounds while he was there. Following his discharge from treatment, Skip became very involved with food and continued to gain weight. When adolescents give up chemicals, some weight gain on getting into the recovery process is normal—and even more so with adolescents who have used amphetamines and other stimulants such as cocaine.

Skip had substituted food for his use of chemicals and had developed a "bonding" or an addictive relationship to food. Skip's weight continued to climb. Efforts to enlist support from Skip's family to intervene on the eating disorder Skip was developing were not very successful, and he continued to gain another thirty pounds within his first eighteen months of sobriety.

One of the major problems confronting the adolescent chemical dependency treatment field is the lack of information provided adolescents regarding sound nutrition. Because chemically dependent adolescents are at high risk for developing eating disorders and because at least 16 percent of these adolescents have eating disorders, we must evaluate what we are presenting to them in treatment for nourishment.

We have to eliminate the junk food and the caffeine and keep fat and sugar to a minimum. Recovering chemically dependent adolescents should not be allowed to have unlimited supplies of junk food. We have to monitor what is being served to them in their meals and what is made available to them in the snack machines.

We have to eliminate the junk food and the caffeine and keep fat and sugar to a minimum.

Adolescents who eat junk food generally do not perform well. Caffeine and sugar stimulate the central nervous system and affect adolescent behavior. If we are sincere in wanting to help these adolescents in gaining control of their behavior, we need to insist on diets that include many complex carbohydrates, fruit, vegetables, lean meat, grains, and very little of the garbage. Often when we change the adolescents' diets, we see a marked improvement in their behavior. And this is not only about weight management; it is about healthy eating habits and how food affects chemically dependent adolescents.

Codependency

Codependency is a difficult term to define inasmuch as few professionals working in this field have been able to reach a consensus on a definition of this disorder. We do know that people who live in dysfunctional families, particularly chemically dependent families, develop a condition known as codependence. We also know that because 57 percent of our chemically dependent adolescents come from alcoholic and drug-addicted families, most of these adolescents will experience problems with codependency.

===

Symptoms of Codependency

Symptoms of codependency in adolescents include the following:

1. They have problems with self-esteem based on a belief that their parents' alcohol and drug or behavior problems are a direct result of the things that these adolescents have done. They believe such things as, "If I were a better person, I could get my parent(s) to stop this. If I had done this or had not done that, they wouldn't drink so much."

2. They assume responsibility for meeting other people's needs, a trait commonly known as "people pleasing," to the extent that they deny their own needs. An example of this is tiptoeing around their active chemically dependent parents in order to keep them from reacting from a hangover. Other examples of this are to refrain from asking their parents to participate in important school events for fear of getting negative responses, and not bringing friends home for fear that they will realize that their family is in trouble.

3. They tend not to understand boundary issues and have a very difficult time with intimacy. Often they have no ability to develop intimate relation-

*ships and refuse to let anybody get deeply in-
volved with them. Even more often, they don't
seem to know where they end and where the next
person begins. They can be inappropriately intrusive in their efforts to socialize and to become
part of a peer group.*

*4. They deny that there is anything wrong in
their famlies or that their parents' alcohol and drug
use has had any impact on them.*

*5. They often show symptoms of PTSD or
anxiety.*

*6. They tend to have psychosomatic and stress-
related illnesses.*

===

Codependent adolescents need to recognize that the ways
in which they see themselves in their relationships to others
are not normal and are based on what they learned in their
families of origin. Family-of-origin issues will continue to
haunt these adolescents into adulthood if we don't confront
them about their codependent issues. These adolescents
need to see that they have altered themselves to fit into a
system that wasn't healthy and that it is not in their best interest to continue this behavior.

It is very uncomfortable sometimes to say to an adolescent, "Your family is not normal and the behavior you have
developed in order to fit into that family is not normal. It
might have worked for you there and it is commendable that
you developed a survival strategy in that family situation, but
it's not working for you out here. The rest of the world isn't
your family and they don't expect this behavior."

Only after we have established relationships with codependent chemically dependent adolescents, and have com-

pleted our evaluations of both the adolescents and their families, can we begin to address codependency. If we see that acting out behavior of these adolescents results directly from their family of origin, we need to confront adolescents with this. I ask them to tell me about people who act like their families do and then ask them, "Does this make sense to you? Do you think that this is how most people live? Is this the way you really want to behave in certain situations?"

Then I confirm with them that this is not normal behavior and it is not what goes on in healthy situations. I ask them, "Is this the kind of relationship you would like to have with your husband and with your kids someday?" And we talk openly and honestly about it.

Codependents fill our helping systems. Many nurses, teachers, therapists, substance abuse counselors, and doctors have suffered from addiction personally, are in codependent relationships, or come from dysfunctional families. These are the personal experiences that lead many of us into this profession and make us "helpers." We learn to be helpers as children. We thought it was our role to fix people.

When we were still very young, we may have known or at least thought that we were good at helping people. These abilities probably grew from codependent behaviors we were developing in trying to control other people in our family or situations, and that behavior remains with many of us. In working with chemically dependent adolescents, we are at high risk.

Those of us who have never experienced codependency personally need to remember that we are still at high risk of developing it as we become involved in long-term relationships with adolescents who are not well. It is very easy to get emotionally invested in these adolescents even when we try to keep our distance.

If you find yourself going home at night thinking about or worrying about an adolescent, you have entered a codependent relationship with that child. This means you may no longer be the best person to help him or her. It also means that it would probably be helpful to you to become involved in a support group such as Al-Anon to learn how to detach from the adolescents with whom you are working. Codependent relationships have developed occasionally between me and adolescents I have worked with in the past, and it will no doubt happen to me again in the future because I have codependent tendencies. We own our own issues and are responsible to get help with our issues. Frankly, I believe that most of us should be in Al-Anon just because we are committed to helping chemically dependent adolescents.

Dual and multiple diagnosed adolescents who are chemically dependent present a high risk for relapse. Chemically dependent adolescents must be assessed and evaluated for disorders other than chemical dependency and their dual or multiple diagnosis issues must be addressed and treated. Treatment plans must be outlined and executed. If we fail to address the dual disorders with conditions as serious as these that have been presented in this chapter, we can see how difficult it would be for adolescents who have these problems to get and stay sober. We quite often find that adolescents who relapse have a dual or multiple diagnosis that has gone undetected or untreated. Therefore, all adolescent chemical dependency treatment centers must be prepared to assess and treat dual diagnosis.

The disorders described in this chapter will not go away nor improve when an adolescent gets into the recovery process. As a matter of fact, the adolescent will find it difficult, if not impossible, to stay sober because of the interference of these other conditions. Both problems, the chemical dependency and the other disorder(s), must be treated simultaneously.

Chapter

5

Diagnosing Adolescent Chemical Dependence

Diagnosis is a process that needs to be completed thoroughly with every adolescent. A diagnosis means that you really evaluate adolescents on all levels. It means that you are able (1) to determine their primary problems, and (2) to communicate this information to adolescents in a way that they understand so that they are able to accept these problems as their own.

The procedure I use has six components: (1) the presenting problem; (2) family assessment; (3) psychosocial history; (4) drug/alcohol use history; (5) addiction symptom checklists; and (6) diagnostic presentation. This process requires six to eight hours if I am to feel confident that I have the information necessary to make an accurate diagnosis.

1. *The Presenting Problem.* Why do adolescents seek help when they do? What motivates them? Have their parents brought them to treatment, did a judge send them, or are they here because they chose to come? Most adolescents are forced by others to get help; therefore, in order to reach adolescents, we must find out why *they* have come to treatment. It may be to get the probation officer off their back. If so, that is one of their presenting problems.

The best way to develop the relationships that you are going to need in order to work effectively with adolescents is to take their presenting problems seriously just the way they give them to you. Don't evaluate them.

I made that mistake early on. A judge would send an adolescent to me and I would ask, "Why are you here today?"

The adolescent would answer, "The judge sent me."

And I would say, "Hey, the judge doesn't just send people over here. Now what's the reason he sent *you*? Doing *drugs*?"

Wrong approach! Harsh confrontation, threats, or challenge will raise denial in adolescents. It usually initiates a power struggle in which adolescents will start challenging you, struggle for control of the session, and not trust you or take you seriously. Harsh confrontation feeds into the adolescent's prepared defenses, making it difficult, if not impossible, to develop an open, honest, and trustful relationship.

A better approach is just to listen to adolescents and take them seriously without analyzing them. You don't have to get everything figured out in this first session. You must develop a relationship first if you expect them to listen to what you have to say later on. You must make the first moves toward mutual respect, trust, and open communication.

The following example demonstrates how I generally approach an adolescent who is sent to me for alcohol and drug use today. In this case, an adolescent boy on probation has been sent by a judge. I start by asking him, "Why are you here?"

When the adolescent says, "The judge sent me," I ask, "Judge Fletcher sent you over here? Do you know why?"

The adolescent usually says, "Nope."

So now I do what I call a "Columbo" approach. I act confused, start looking through files and forms on my desk, and say, "Well, *that's* interesting. I wonder why he sent you here and not to the mental health center?"

The adolescent says, "I don't know."

I say, "Wait a minute while I call him and find out what this is all about."

Now the adolescent says, "All right, I got an OMVI!" (Operating a Motor Vehicle Intoxicated).

That's usually the first step. Then I say, "You mean you think he sent you over here *just* because you were picked up for an OMVI?"

"Yeah."

So I say, "OK. One of your problems is that the judge is all over you. Right?"

"Right."

"And he's all over you because you've got an OMVI. Right?"

"Right."

"Anything else?" And I proceed with getting information from the adolescent by warming him up to me. I take him seriously, I don't evaluate or criticize what he says, and I dont' drop into a critical adult mode with him. I may say, "That's interesting. Something like that happened to me when I was a kid too. Craziest thing!"

This is the best place to start with adolescents. By the end of session one, I usually have not mentioned drugs. I just don't do it. If you want to lower their defenses, don't discuss their drugs. Discuss the things that they perceive as problems. Those are the things you are going to use to motivate them to seek treatment.

"So you want the judge off your back. You want a better relationship with your girl friend. You want your driver's license back." I have them tell me what's important to *them.* That's how you approach presenting problems. That's where you grab adolescents: What motivates them, not what motivates their parents or a judge.

Presenting problems are whatever adolescents present to you—the whole list, even down to "my girl friend's nagging me all the time." If it is important to them, it goes down in "presenting problems." Then you read it back to them at the end of the session so they know you have been listening to them.

2. *Family assessment.* An important piece of the diagnostic process is to find out about the functioning level of this adolescent's family. What is happening in this family and what is the adolescent's role in the family? Right up front, I find out about the family's chemical use history and their beliefs about chemicals, including alcohol. The family assessment should be made at the same time as the adolescent's. I prefer to have the family work with a different therapist to prevent me from getting triangled in the family system.

3. *Brief psychosocial history.* Get a basic story. I ask adolescents to tell me something about what they were like as small children. They generally will say something like "I don't know. I wasn't there."

I then ask them, "What do people *say* you were like as a little kid? What were you like in grade school? What were you involved in? What did you like and what didn't you like? What was the best thing that ever happened to you? What was the worst thing?" Get the adolescent to name significant events.

Try to get a feeling of what kind of family system adolescents belong to from their point of view. Then you will start feeling you know these adolescents. If you've shared a little about yourself with them, they won't feel as defensive with you.

4. *Drug and alcohol use history.* Start to explore the alcohol and drug use history, but only after you've accomplished the first three procedures; then these questions won't seem as invading. In my experience it is rare that I've asked

the first drug-use question. It is almost always divulged spontaneously. If you sit through a session or two and never mention chemicals while looking at the rest of their problems, most adolescents will want to find out what you think of their chemical use.

If I stay off the chemical issue, most adolescents will bring it up themselves. For example, by the end of the first session, some adolescents will say, "And I do drink a little." I ignore it. Or they say, "And I smoke pot once in a while." And I ignore it. They wonder if I have heard them.

Typically, I will say, "Let's get back to what's going on with your girl friend." Sometimes adolescents will leave the first session thinking, "Maybe my drug use is not that big of a deal?"

In the second session I'm back to talking about their girl friends or boyfriends, the judge, the OMVIs, what they were like as young children, and about their family. I need to have this information anyway to make an accurate diagnosis. Usually during the second session adolescents will say to me, "and I've done 'acid,' 'speed,' and 'ludes' and. . ." Now they want my attention. They want to know, "Is this normal?"

I say, "Is *this* what you want to talk about? Drug use? Fine. Tell me about it"—almost as if it's an inconvenience. That's the way to start. Not all adolescents will do this, but most of them will.

Making a Chemical Dependency or "C.D." Diagnosis

When adolescents are using chemicals at all, they will fit into one of four categories: (a) experimental use, (b) psychosocial dependence, (c) harmful use, or (d) core addiction.

a. *Experimental use* is self-explanatory. They want to know what liquor tastes like and how it makes you feel; what it is like to get drunk and to be drunk. Considering that most of the adolescents in this society who graduate from high school claim to have smoked marijuana, it is clear that the majority of them simply wanted to know what it was like to smoke and to be high on pot.

This is not something that they do every time they go out to a party or that they need in order to have a good time. They simply want to find out what using chemicals is all about, the same way they want to find out about dating, sex, and other things in the world. This is not abnormal behavior nor does it indicate an adolescent who needs treatment.

Is there a problem then with experimental use? Should we be telling adolescents who we know are not chemically dependent and do not have a genetic background of chemical dependency—meaning that somebody in their family is alcoholic or drug dependent—not to drink at all? Yes, we should because (1) it is against the law and (2) it interferes with normal adolescent development. All adolescent treatment providers, whether they are psychiatric or substance abuse professionals, need to take the position that no one should be drinking or using drugs *at all* during adolescence.

Adolescents who are caught in the experimental use stage do not need to be in a treatment program of any kind, not even outpatient. They need alcohol and drug information and discouragement from further drinking or drug use. This should be handled by trained professionals within the school system through substance abuse education, prevention, and intervention programs.

b. *Psychosocial dependence.* These are adolescents who use alcohol and drugs to help them accomplish something that they believe they couldn't do without chemicals. An example of this is a social drinker who says, ''I can't get out on the dance floor until I've had a couple of drinks.'' That's a psychosocially dependent statement. It means that person is psychosocially dependent on alcohol in order to do something.

Adolescents start to become psychosocially dependent on alcohol or marijuana when they use them to be able to do certain things. Maybe they feel they have to have a few drinks to ask somebody out on a date or maybe to go out on that date. Psychosocial dependence means chemicals are starting to pose a problem. When adolescents start bonding with a chemical in several life areas in order to accomplish something, they may be well on their way to addiction. These adolescents are not addicted yet. Adolescents in this stage need extensive education and evaluation.

If there is no genetic history of chemical dependency and it doesn't appear that the adolescent's psychosocial dependence is very serious, then it can be dealt with through outpatient drug and alcohol intervention, education, and values clarification to stop continued chemical use. But there should be an assessment and intervention if adolescents are further into their chemical use than previously suspected.

c. **Harmful use.** This category pertains to adolescents who have become so involved with chemicals that they depend on them to cope, rather than coping with life as it is without chemicals. These adolescents use chemicals to the point that they are compromising important aspects of their lives, such as their education, family, health, and/or their role in the community. They are often getting into trouble.

These adolescents are paying consequences for their use of chemicals in important ways. They have all the symptoms of chemical dependency except withdrawal. They have developed **tolerance,** which means that it takes more of the chemical now for them to achieve the high that they're after than it did when they first began using. They have all the symptoms of **progression,** meaning they use greater amounts of chemicals more frequently with higher costs in consequences. They may or may not have a genetic link, but they have all the symptoms of chemical dependency. At this point, they still do not have **withdrawal,** meaning that when they stop using the chemical they don't seem to suffer for it physically.

This is chemical dependency and often responds well to intensive outpatient treatment.

d. *Core addiction.* These adolescents have the chronic, primary disease of chemical addiction that usually has a genetic basis and is prone to relapse. Their use of chemicals has impaired them in major life areas; they have developed tolerance; and they experience withdrawal. Both harmful use and core addiction are chemical dependency and should be treated as such. The main difference is that, in core addiction adolescents will experience physical withdrawal. Withdrawal is dangerous and should be medically managed on an inpatient unit.

In evaluating chemical dependency, you first complete an alcohol and drug use history. You go back to the beginning and find out how and when adolescents started using chemicals. It is important to know with whom they drank or took drugs, why they were doing it, how much they used, and how often. In diagnosing chemical dependency you need to find out about the situations related to these adolescents' chemical use. What is it that they can't cope with? What are they trying to avoid or accomplish by using chemicals?

Adolescents' drug and alcohol use histories should give you a pretty good idea as to which one of the four categories they fit into even before you use addiction symptom checklists. And I believe it is important that you put them into one of these four categories, if for no other reason than to standardize the terminology that you are going to use with other professionals with whom you work.

When you say, "This adolescent is psychosocially dependent and needs drug and alcohol education and further evaluation rather than treatment at this point," other professionals will understand what you are talking about.

Next we use addiction symptom checklists to verify our findings.

5. *Addiction symptom checklists.* When I have fully explored the adolescent's drug and alcohol use history, I follow that up with addiction symptom checklists, which are used to confirm or to rule out the diagnosis you've already made.

Addiction symptom checklists developed to evaluate adolescent chemical use will be far more helpful than adult instruments. Two assessment instruments for adolescents that I use regularly and recommend are the "Nelson Symptom Checklist" (Nelson) and the "Adolescent Alcohol Involvement Scale" (AAIS, Mayer and Filstead). The use of these symptom checklists is explained in the following section on "Using Tools Designed for Diagnosing Adolescent Chemical Dependency." These symptom checklists should be used by a counselor, with the adolescent present. They are **not** valid when used as a homework assignment for the adolescent to complete alone.

6. *Diagnostic presentation.* Finally, I make the diagnostic presentation—first to the adolescents and then to the adolescents with their parents. I always try to instill hope in adolescents throughout the diagnostic process. I tell them, "We're working toward a diagnostic presentation. Between now and then, we are going to spend a lot of time together. I'm going to have to get a lot of information from you and you have tests to take." Adolescents understand tests and they want to know what their scores are on tests. They want to know, "How am I doing?"

I tell them, "Well, you can't really know from just one test. We've got to put them all together. But before your folks or anybody else knows, I'm going to share with you just how you scored on all this." Now they are into the process *with* me.

After I have gathered all the data and I know the results,

then I start bracing the adolescent for the diagnosis. Adolescents should know what their problems are, because if they don't know what their problems are they can't work on them. Throughout the process, I am leading adolescents up to the big day when they find out what is causing their problems, and they really get into this.

As I build them up to the final result, if their problem is chemical dependency, I am giving them a little drug and alcohol education along the way. I am saying things that cause them to do a little internal searching. No challenges; just using their own words and rephrasing them in ways that cause them to see that what they have been doing was violating their principles all along.

I say things to them like, "Tell me, what is your definition of a 'social drinker,' 'an abuser,' and 'an addict'? I want your definition of those three things." Typically adolescents' ideas of social users are themselves. When asked to define a "social user," they usually describe themselves. I ask these adolescents, "Does your description seem to be a little too heavy a use of chemicals to be 'social'?"

Usually the adolescent will say, "Well, no."

Then I ask, "Didn't you tell me your mother was a social drinker? Does she drink like that?"

"No. OK. My mom's a social user and I'm an abuser."

Then I ask, "What's the difference between an 'abuser' and an 'addict'?"

The adolescent's typical response is, "An addict has to have drugs every minute of every day of his life."

And I say, "Now wait a minute. Remember that guy that came in to talk to the group one day who was telling you about his addiction? Wasn't he a lawyer? He used to go all day for many days without drugs, and yet he said he was an addict, didn't he?"

"Yeah."

"So maybe it's not true that being an addict means using

drugs every minute of every day. As a matter of fact, you've met recovering folks since you've been coming here. Is being an addict having to have drugs every minute of every day?"

"No, I guess not." Then adolescents will usually say things like, "Gee, I think I must be right 'on the line.'" And that's far enough for now.

At the diagnostic presentation point, it is enough to get them to admit, "I'm seriously involved and I'm past the point of just abuse and my control strategies have failed." They don't have to say, "I'm a drug addict." They recognize, "I'm seriously impaired by my chemical use." That is the starting point. Now you are ready to start talking formal treatment to them, but not before they have arrived at this point. What would motivate them? They think they can still control it.

After you have made the diagnostic presentation to the adolescent, then you say, "Look, we've got to call your parents in and tell them about this." You explain to the adolescent that you will do this same diagnostic presentation all over again for the family with him or her present.

I recommend that, out of respect, adolescents be given the results first and that they should be present when you tell the parents. It is their life and they mentally have to start deciding how they are going to interact with Mom and Dad once their parents receive this information.

Using Tools Designed for
Diagnosing Adolescent Chemical Dependency

Standardization of Terms. It is very important to standardize the terms you use in making your assessment of an adolescent and in documenting your diagnosis. Various symptom checklists use different names for certain symptoms and levels of chemical use. When using these assessment tools, the different names used to describe similar symptoms must be translated back to standardized terms.

For example, in the Nelson Chart, the term "Experimental

Use" correlates with the term "Normal Chemical Use by Adolescents" used in the Adolescent Alcohol Involvement Scale (AAIS). If you determine that an adolescent is in the "Experimental Use" or "Normal Use" stage from using these symptom checklists, your diagnosis should be translated back to experimental use because this is the term that is most accepted in the profession.

Nelson refers to psychosocial dependence as "more regular use" and the AAIS calls this stage "heavy users." A diagnosis of this level on either checklist should be translated back to "psychosocial dependence" on the adolescent's diagnostic evaluation. Nelson calls Harmful Use, "daily pre-occupation" and the AAIS calls it "alcohol misuse." If this is where you evaluate an adolescent to be, you need to translate that back to "Harmful Use." Finally, Nelson calls Core Addiction "dependency" and the AAIS calls this stage "alcoholic-like drinkers." Again, if you arrive at scores in those categories, you need to translate that back to "Core Addiction" for your diagnosis.

===

Stages of Adolescent Chemical Use
Nelson's Chart, 1978

STAGE 1: EXPERIMENTAL USE

[ ] *1. Occasional chemical use (mostly beer or marijuana), usually on weekends or during the summer, predominantly with friends.*

[ ] *2. There is low tolerance; adolescent becomes intoxicated easily.*

[ ] *3. Feeling grown up and defying parents as part of the high.*

[ ] *4. Use often unplanned; alcohol or drugs sneaked from home.*

[ ] *5. Harder drugs (speed, LSD, barbiturates, angel dust) are little used at this stage.*

STAGE 2: MORE REGULAR USE

[ ] *1. Increase in tolerance. More parties involving alcohol. Feeling that "everyone does it" and wanting to be part of that. Staying out late at night or all night.*

[ ] *2. More money spent. Use of false ID's. Alcohol bought and shared with friends.*

[ ] *3. Beer and marijuana remain drugs of choice, although use of harder liquor may increase.*

[ ] *4. Parents become aware of use and attempt to contain the adolescent's chemical use through stringent rules and punishments.*

[ ] *5. Increase in consumption, along with pride in being able to "handle it."*

[ ] *6. Alcohol or drug-using friends are often not introduced to parents.*

[ ] *7. Use of alcohol and drugs during the week begins. School skipping may increase as well as dropping school activities and sports. Grades may drop.*

[ ] *8. Blackouts may begin to occur.*

[ ] *9. Parents are lied to about the extent of alcohol and drug use and the money being spent on alcohol and drugs.*

[ ] *10. Solitary use begins. Adolescent tries to fool parents or teachers when intoxicated.*

[ ] *11. Non-alcohol and non-drug-using friends*

dropped. Parties may now occur which last the entire weekend.

[   ] 12. Preoccupation with chemical use begins. Next drinking session is carefully planned for and anticipated. Concern develops over source of supply.

[   ] 13. Use during the day begins. Use of drugs other than alcohol and marijuana begins on a regular basis.

STAGE 3:   DAILY PREOCCUPATION

[   ] 1. Increase in the use of harder drugs (speed, LSD, barbiturates, angel dust).

[   ] 2. Dealing or fronting for others may begin.

[   ] 3. Increase in the number of times high during the week. Amount of money spent on alcohol and other drugs increases.

[   ] 4. Decrease in social use. Getting "loaded" rather than just high becomes the goal. Being intoxicated becomes common and "normal."

[   ] 5. May be legal trouble for minor consumption or possession. Possible arrest for driving while intoxicated.

[   ] 6. More alcohol and drugs are bought and used. Alcohol and drugs become the center of the adolescent's activities.

[   ] 7. Adolescent may attempt to cut down or stop to demonstrate control.

[   ] 8. Possible stealing to get money for alcohol or drugs.

[   ] 9. Most non-drug-using friends are dropped.

[   ] 10. Solitary use increases further. Adolescent isolates self even from friends that use.

[ ] 11. Possible increase in money owed for alcohol and drugs.
[ ] 12. Lying about or hiding supply of alcohol and drugs.
[ ] 13. More school truancy and trouble with parents over use.

STAGE 4: DEPENDENCY

[ ] 1. Drinking and drug use at school and at work. Alcohol or drugs are needed to face the day. Alcohol or drugs are used to escape the uncomfortable feelings that result from excessive alcohol and drug use.
[ ] 2. Increased guilt. Questioning own use but unable to control it.
[ ] 3. Possible use of injectable drugs.
[ ] 4. Friends are "burn-outs" (seriously impaired from alcohol and drug abuse) and may be proud of it.
[ ] 5. Adolescent is unable to determine what normal behavior is. Being high has become the norm. During periods of abstinence the adolescent is confused and unable to think clearly.
[ ] 6. Poor self-image; self-hate develops. Casual sexual involvement begins. Denial of problem continues.
[ ] 7. Dropping out of school. Possibly more police involvement. Parents may give up at this point and abandon efforts to intervene. Victimization may begin during periods of intoxication.
[ ] 8. Worsening physical condition. Weight loss, more frequent sickness, poor memory.

[ ] 9. *Suicidal thoughts and tendencies may occur.*

[ ] 10. *Increase in paranoia. Most money goes for alcohol and drug use.*

[ ] 11. *Loss of control over use occurs and continues to grow worse.*

—Reprinted from Illinois Alcoholism Counselor Certification Board, Inc., 104 N. 4th St., Springfield, IL, Unit 1, pages 75-78, 1983.

===

Stages of Adolescent Chemical Use
Nelson's Chart, 1978

INTERPRETATION

(Interpretations are made by Terence T. Gorski based on the Nelson Chart.)

Stage 1: Experimental Use: Adolescents are prone to experiment with alcohol and drugs. Simple experimentation should be responded to by entering the child into alcohol and drug abuse education and prevention programs.

Stage 2: More Regular Use: This does not indicate dependence. It should be considered an indicator that the adolescent needs alcohol and drug abuse counseling. Outpatient services would typically be sufficient and should be attempted and failed prior to an inpatient treatment.

> *Special concern should be given to adolescents in this stage who have biological parents who are chemically dependent due to the increased genetic risk factors.*

> **Stage 3:** *Daily Preoccupation: This is a definitive sign of chemical dependence in the adolescent. Inpatient treatment is typically recommended due to the high levels of denial, the undermining of alcohol and drug-centered peers, the presence of obsession and compulsion which blocks self-awareness, and the state of confusion that typically occurs during periods of abstinence.*

> **Stage 4:** *The adolescent is incapacitated by alcohol. Intervention strategies should be used to force entry into inpatient rehabilitation. Physical illness may need to be treated. Major rehabilitation may be required dependent upon the extent of alcohol and drug-related damage to the personality.*

Both the Nelson Chart and AAIS are symptom checklists, designed to determine the degree or *stage* of chemical involvement by the adolescent. One thing to remember in working with these instruments is that you need to use both Nelson and AAIS.

1. *The Nelson Chart.*

The Nelson Chart, "Stages of Adolescent Chemical Use," shows the *progression* of chemical involvement. It will show you how far adolescents have come in their experimental use along the scale toward core addiction. This tool will help you to visualize in your mind a line from the first drinking episode to core addiction. Nelson breaks progression into four stages: (1) experimental use; (2) more regular use; (3) daily preoccupation; and (4) dependency.

Nelson has done a good job with this; however, there is one major problem I have found in working with this instrument. In some areas where you can make only one check mark, he's measuring more than one thing. For example, in Stage Two, "More Regular Use," in Item No. 1, Nelson asks us to check (a) "increased tolerance," (b) "more parties involving alcohol," or (c) "feeling that everyone does this." Each of these options is measuring a different thing.

People often ask, "What do I check when the adolescent has some of the behaviors described in a question but not all of them?" This requires a judgment call. If the adolescent's answer is 51 percent, yes, check it. If it is less than that, don't check it. After you have checked everything that applies to the adolescent you are evaluating, you then turn to the interpretation key and circle the appropriate answer. By applying the interpretation to what you have checked, you will see how far adolescents have progressed in their chemical use.

If they have checked off only one answer in one of the categories, that does not mean that they have moved into that category. For example, if they have experienced most of the items in Stage Two and only one item in Stage Three, they may be in transition but are currently still in Stage Two.

Finally, you read the results to yourself and then translate Nelson's terms back to one of the four standardized categories of adolescent chemical use. Addiction is basically stepping over that invisible line from "social use" to "addiction," and exactly *when* that happens is seldom definite. However, using this instrument will enable you to see how it's happening.

2. *"The Adolescent Alcohol Involvement Scale" (AAIS).*

In using Nelson, you can use the words "alcohol" and

"drugs" interchangeably, but not on this one. The AAIS focuses on alcohol. It is very well designed and has been thoroughly field tested and evaluated. You are free to use this instrument, and I recommend you do because I think it is the more solid of these two instruments. All that the developers of the AAIS, Mayer and Filstead, ask in return is that you register with them first. To do this, you may write to them at the address printed at the end of the test, explain how you learned of the AAIS and how you are using it. As they do more research, they may want to call on folks who are using this instrument to get feedback.

In using the AAIS, you circle *everything* that applies to the adolescent you are evaluating. Sometimes there will be more than one answer to a question, and you circle the numbers of all answers that apply. Next you turn to the scoring procedure. You mark the score for each category to the right of the score sheet, but you do not add up the numerical values of the items you circled.

For example, if in question one, you circled No. 2 and No. 4, the total score is *4,* not 6. The score in each category is the highest *number* of the item marked with that category, but you don't add them together. After you have scored each category, use the scoring procedure to arrive at the total score.

When you have completed the AAIS and scored it, consolidate symptom checklists. If you have completed the first four steps of the diagnostic process and these two checklists, you will know which one of the four categories of chemical use applies to the adolescent you are evaluating. You should be able to rule out or diagnose chemical dependency at this point.

When you've pulled together all the data you have gathered in your evaluation, you are able to prepare your diagnostic presentation in a professional manner using standardized terms and to document your findings based on these instruments.

Your evaluation might say: "My diagnosis is that this child shows harmful use. Nelson rates this child in the last stages which I think is questionable because he doesn't have physical withdrawal. I am also diagnosing harmful use since it is certain that this child has **chemical dependency** without **physical withdrawal**. The AAIS score was consistent with this.

"This child comes from a dysfunctional family where the mother is an alcoholic. In addition to being chemically dependent, he is also an ACOA (adult child of an alcoholic), which means that he has codependency issues. Based on the psychosocial history, there is also possible depression. However, because I cannot validate that, I'm going to ask for a consultation. This child is delayed in only a few areas of his normal adolescent development, those areas being primarily in impulse control due to his inability as yet to understand the concept of time."

This is the kind of presentation that I will want to make.

When you have completed your six- or seven-hour diagnostic process, you are now able to say, "My recommendations for treatment based on these data are either that (1) we admit the child to a substance abuse program, or (2) we keep him in a regular school program and make sure he attends drug and alcohol education"; or whatever else your recommendations are, based on your diagnosis.

You cannot realistically help someone if you do not have a thorough diagnosis. You cannot simply sit and talk to an adolescent, let them tell you their problems, and then say, "This is what we are going to do for you." Your problem list and your treatment plans need to be based on the information you get through the assessment and diagnosis process. This will help you avoid being manipulated into things that are not real or are based in the adolescent's pathology.

We can set ourselves up for this if we are not operating on hard information. Our "gut" alone isn't good enough. Mine never was. Without these steps, our treatment plans will be ineffective. All the avenues will be left open for us to make serious mistakes with adolescents if we don't use consistent tools. We need to have a strategy for obtaining the kinds of information we need to gather and for what we are going to do with that information.

==

Adolescent Alcohol Involvement Scale (AAIS)
John Mayer and William J. Filstead

Questionnaire

1. How often do you drink?
  A. Never.
  B. Once or twice a year.
  C. Once or twice a month.
  D. Every weekend.
  E. Several times a week.
  F. Every day.

2. When did you have your last drink?
  A. Never drank.
  B. Not for over a year.
  C. Between six months and one year ago.
  D. Several weeks ago.
  E. Last week.
  F. Yesterday.
  G. Today.

3. I usually start to drink because:
  A. I like the taste.
  B. I want to be like my friends.

C. I want to feel like an adult.

D. I feel nervous, tense, full of worries or problems.

E. I feel sad, lonely, sorry for myself.

4. What do you drink?
    A. Wine.
    B. Beer.
    C. Mixed drinks.
    D. Hard liquor.
    E. A substitute for alcohol: paint thinner, sterno, cough medicine, mouthwash, hair tonic, etc.

5. How do you get your drinks?
    A. Supervised by parents or relatives.
    B. From brothers or sisters.
    C. From home without parent's knowledge.
    D. From friends.
    E. Buy it with false identification.

6. When did you take your first drink?
    A. Never.
    B. Recently.
    C. After age 15.
    D. At ages 14 or 15.
    E. Between ages 10 to 13.
    F. Before age 10.

7. What time of day do you usually drink?
    A. With meals.
    B. At night.
    C. Afternoon.

D. Mostly in the morning or when I first awake.

E. I often get up during my sleep and drink.

8. Why did you take your first drink?
   A. Curiosity.
   B. Parents or relatives offered.
   C. Friends encouraged me.
   D. To feel more like an adult.
   E. To get drunk or high.

9. How much do you drink, when you do drink?
   A. One drink.
   B. Two drinks.
   C. Three to six drinks.
   D. Six or more drinks.
   E. Until "High or Drunk."

10. Whom do you drink with?
    A. Parents or relatives only.
    B. With brothers or sisters only.
    C. With friends own age.
    D. With older friends.
    E. Alone.

11. What is the greatest effect you have had from alcohol?
    A. Loose easy feeling.
    B. Moderately "high."
    C. Drunk.
    D. Became ill.
    E. Passed out.
    F. When drinking heavily and the next day didn't remember what happened.

117

12. **What is the greatest effect drinking has had on your life?**
    A. None, no effect.
    B. Has interfered with talking to someone.
    C. Has prevented me from having a good time.
    D. Has interfered with my schoolwork.
    E. Have lost friends because of drinking.
    F. Has gotten me into trouble at home.
    G. Was in a fight which destroyed property.
    H. Has resulted in an accident, an injury, arrest, or being punished at school for drinking.

13. **How do you feel about your drinking?**
    A. No problem at all.
    B. I can control it and set limits for myself.
    C. I can control myself, but my friends influence me.
    D. I often feel bad about my drinking.
    E. I need help to control myself.
    F. I have had professional help to control my drinking.

14. **How do others see you?**
    A. Can't say, or, a normal drinker for my age.
    B. When I drink, I tend to neglect my family and friends.
    C. My family or friends advise me to control or cut down on my drinking.
    D. My family or friends tell me to get help for my drinking.
    E. My family or friends have already gone for help for my drinking.

Adolescent Alcohol Involvement Scale (AAIS)
John Mayer and William J. Filstead

Scoring Procedure

(This scoring system was developed by Terence T. Gorski.)

Scoring Instructions: Review the completed questionnaire and circle the numerical score that corresponds to the checked answer. Enter the number of the circled item in the column labeled *Score.* Total the scores and enter in the appropriate box. Turn to the interpretations on the following page.

Question:	A	B	C	D	E	F	G	H	Score
1	0	2	3	4	5	6			
2	0	2	3	4	5	6	7		
3	1	2	3	4	5				
4	1	2	3	4	5				
5	1	2	3	4	5				
6	0	2	3	4	5	6			
7	1	2	3	4	5				
8	1	2	3	4	5				
9	1	2	3	4	5				
10	1	2	3	4	5				

11	1	2	3	4	5	6		
12	0	2	3	4	5	6	7	8
13	0	2	3	4	5	6		
14	0	2	3	4	5			

TOTAL SCORE:

Adolescent Alcohol Involvement Scale (AAIS)
John Mayer and William J. Filstead

Interpretation

Interpretation: Compare the total score to the score ranges listed below.

Adolescent heavy users MAY require outpatient services for education and prevention. If there is a coexisting adolescent disorder, outpatient therapy will be indicated.

Adolescent misusers will typically require in-patient treatment followed by outpatient services. Length of stay will be determined by the presence and severity of coexisting adolescent disorders.

Normal Adolescents:
0   Total abstainer (11.36%).
1-19   Rarely uses alcohol (9.32%).

Adolescent Heavy Users:
20-41   Adolescents who drink but do not have alcohol-related behavior problems (60.24%).

Adolescent Misuers:
42-57   Alcohol misuse (15.07%).
58-79   Alcoholic-like drinkers (4%).

===

William J. Filstead, Parkside Lutheran Hospital, 1700 Park Ridge Road, Park Ridge, IL 60068.

Chapter
6

The Adolescent Developmental Model of Recovery

Recovery is the process of learning to live a comfortable and meaningful life sober. Abstinence alone is not enough. To achieve lasting sobriety, a chemically dependent adolescent needs to be abstinent *plus* pass through stages of a recovery process.

A **developmental process** is a series of progressive stages that lead people from basic skills to sophisticated capabilities, such as those children must go through in learning to walk. Before they can begin to learn to walk, children must first learn how to sit up and to keep their backs straight. Then they have to learn to stand, first holding on to something, and then to stand alone. Next, children learn to balance their gait in taking steps forward. That's the foundation children need to have in order to walk. And they have to learn to walk before they can run, and to run before they can skip.

With chemically dependent adolescents, the foundation for recovery is abstinence. Abstinence is a first and constant requirement for sobriety; but sobriety and abstinence are not the same thing. Sobriety is abstinence *plus* the recovery process.

Many chemically dependent adolescents go through

periods we call **controlled abstinence** during their active addictive phase. They swear off all alcohol and drugs for a few weeks, and some may remain abstinent for months. They are still in the midst of their addiction, however, in terms of their personalities and their life-styles. People in AA call this "white knuckling" it. These adolescents are just holding on—minute by minute, day by day, and week by week—trying not to use, while in their minds they are planning their next use. They know that eventually they are going to use chemicals again.

When adolescents say, "I'm not using anymore and it makes me miserable," that's not recovery. It's only abstinence without the recovery process. When they say, "I'm not using chemicals and I'm growing, learning and working at staying sober; I'm involved in a process of making changes and my life is getting better," these are signs of recovery leading to lasting and comfortable sobriety.

Abstinence alone is not enough. A chemically dependent adolescent needs to be abstinent plus pass through stages of a recovery process."

Recovery actually *starts,* however, before the chemically dependent adolescent decides to abstain from using all alcohol and drugs. It begins with the addiction process itself and the pain and frustration that addiction causes. Recovery begins when adolescents start learning through the laws of consequences that they cannot safely use alcohol or drugs. They begin to move ahead in recovery when they decide to learn to live a meaningful and comfortable way of life without chemicals.

The "Adolescent Model of Recovery" (ADMR) is based on the work of Terence T. Gorski, who developed the "Adult Developmental Model of Recovery." What I have done is adapt that model for use with adolescents.

The Adolescent Developmental
Model of Recovery

The "Adolescent Developmental Model of Recovery" (ADMR) is based on first laying a foundation in abstinence and then building steps on which to complete more complicated tasks in recovery. The ADMR is a road map for recovery for chemically dependent adolescents. It describes where recovery starts and explains the steps that must be followed to achieve lasting sobriety.

Adolescents must progress in an orderly fashion from stage to stage in the ADMR process. They cannot go from Stage "A" to Stage "D." If they don't complete each of the stages in order, they do not develop the skills necessary to successfully complete the higher level tasks that will be required further on in their recovery programs. Just as children may not be able to skip because they didn't master one of the basics in learning to walk, adolescents can't be comfortable and productive while sober if they don't build their foundation skills first.

Recovering chemically dependent adults start with abstinence and then move into recovery and sobriety. Chemically dependent adolescents are also moving from childhood through adolescence to adulthood. They are moving through two developmental processes at the same time. This complicates the issues that they will have to deal with in recovery.

The ADMR provides a checklist which can be used to follow adolescents' progress in recovery and to verify that they are doing what they need to do to stay sober. It helps adolescents to recognize where they are in the recovery process and when they are stuck in their recovery. It helps them to see what they should be working on and what their treatment goals should be. The ADMR will also help adolescents to understand factors that complicate their recovery and that lead to the relapse process.

The ADMR will help counselors to develop appropriate treatment plans for adolescents. It will also help parents to have realistic expectations for the progress of their recovering adolescents.

There are six phases in the Adolescent ADMR: (1) pretreatment, (2) stabilization, (3) early recovery, (4) middle recovery, (5) late recovery, (6) maintenance.

Pretreatment

Pretreatment is the last stage of active use of chemicals and the first stage of recovery. In this phase chemically dependent adolescents begin (1) to acknowledge the consequences of their chemical use; (2) to struggle with issues of control, meaning that they give up the need to control their chemical use; and (3) to accept the fact that abstinence without life-style changes is not a viable option.

The **pretreatment tasks of the ADMR** are (1) to develop a history of problems related to addiction; (2) to recognize a pattern of addiction-related problems; (3) to attempt controlled use; (4) to attempt abstinence without help; (5) to experience a motivational crisis; and (6) to agree to enter appropriate treatment.

The pretreatment phase begins with adolescents experiencing consequences as a result of their chemical use. They finally begin to examine their use of chemicals when consequences start being imposed on them because of it. They go into what I call **control modes.** The three modes of controlling drinking or drug use are (1) **limiting** the amount or frequency of chemical use; (2) **changing** the kinds of chemicals used; and (3) **attempting abstinence** without help to get people "off their backs."

Adolescents say, "From now on, I'm not using on school nights, only on the weekend. I'm only going to one party a week." Or they'll say, "I'm getting off the hard stuff, the cocaine and the 'ludes, and I'm going back to using just 'pot' and alcohol," or, "I'm not going to use hard liquor anymore. I'm just going to drink beer."

Adolescents start saying and doing these kinds of things to prove to themselves and everybody else that they can control their use of chemicals. At this point, they often don't have enough evidence to prove them wrong.

When adolescents try these controlled-use patterns and fail, they will often attempt **controlled abstinence.** They'll say, "I'm swearing off all booze and drugs just to prove to everybody that I can quit any time I want to. I'm not using anything for the next six weeks." Sometimes they will go for weeks at a time without using chemicals, but many times they can't. So they say, "Well, I just changed my mind."

When this kind of thinking and planning is present, adolescents are entering the final stages of their active use. They are finally evaluating the impact the chemicals are having on them and trying "scientific experiments" to prove that they can either control their use of alcohol or drugs or stop using altogether. These are positive signs that they are going to be "treatment ready" soon. They will not stay in recovery long if they have not struggled with these issues.

Chemically dependent adolescents who still believe there are chemicals that they can control are doomed to try them. As long as they still believe that there are ways to control their chemical use, they are compelled to go back and try them, including attempts at controlled abstinence. The fact that adolescents are not using does not mean they are in recovery. It may mean they are still in the "control" part of the pretreatment stage.

An important part of the evaluation process is to see if chemically dependent adolescents have dealt with control issues. If they are saying, "I know I can control it," we ask them how they know that. How have they tried to control it in the past? When they are using these strategies, we know they have entered the pretreatment stage.

It is frustrating when adolescents are still saying that they can control their chemical use, but the fact that they have implemented strategies to control their use means that, in spite of their denial, they know they have a problem. You don't have to control how often you eat green beans; you have to control only the things that cause problems. *One of the first tasks of the pretreatment stage is to develop a history of problems related to the addiction.*

Once adolescents have identified their chemical use as a problem, it becomes possible to work with them toward recovery. If they have never instituted control strategies, then either the consequences of their use are nonexistent or minimal or they don't yet understand the connection between their chemical use and the consequences.

Adolescents need to connect the consequences they are experiencing as being directly related to their drug and alcohol use. Often they need help to see this, but if they don't have the "aha!—that's it!," they will continue to see everything as unrelated and in compartments.

At first they'll say, "Bad things happen to me because I have bad luck," or "Things happen to me because I'm just a bad kid," or "My whole family's like this: Everything happens to us; we never get a break." The adolescent has to see, "No, that's not the issue. If I wasn't using chemicals, this wouldn't happen."

I don't make it a practice to tell adolescents this. Instead, I guide them through a series of exercises to help them come to terms with the fact that the common denominator in the bad things happening in their lives is their drug use. It will mean more if it comes from them, if they experience that "Aha! It's the booze! It's the drugs!" moment of truth.

All of a sudden one day chemically dependent adolescents put this together. They'll say, "The reason I can't get along with my parents is my drug use. Every time I've been out partying all weekend and have drugs in my system, I act out. That's when my mom and I get into it." Or, "Every time I go on binges I get into trouble and get kicked out of school," or "It was my drug use that ruined my last relationship!"

Adolescents need to come to these conclusions for themselves. They therefore need to have a history of problems related to their addictions to make the pretreatment piece of this work. Then they have to *recognize the pattern of addiction-related problems* and see that all of these problems (1) continue to get worse and (2) have a common denominator—alcohol and/or drugs.

Next, adolescents need to *attempt controlled use of chemicals,* such as limiting the frequency and quantity of their use or changing the substances they use. When this fails, they will *attempt abstinence without support.* They will say, "I can fix this by simply not using. That's it, and now I won't have any more problems!" Adolescents who are chemically dependent will fail at this too because they are practicing abstinence without making necessary attitude and life-style changes. Eventually, they will get into a stressful situation or be uncomfortable at a party, and they will use again.

Adolescents need to experience a motivational crisis in the pretreatment stage. This may be in the form of trouble with the law or getting expelled from schoool; something that's very important to them has to be on the line due to their chemical use. They may have had their driver's license suspended, been kicked off the football team, or dumped by their boyfriend or girl friend. Only after these kinds of things have happened to them are they ready to agree to enter appropriate treatment and begin recovery.

The first step then is to move adolescents into pretreatment because they can't start recovery without it. They have to understand that they cannot control chemicals. If they attempt recovery before this happens they will be complying only to get you out of their hair so that they can get back to their chemicals.

We all hear stories about adolescents who go through treatment programs and are using drugs again the day they are discharged, and this is why. These adolescents may have been model patients in the treatment center when they were forced to go in, but in their minds they did not believe they were chemically dependent. They did not yet believe they could not control chemicals. They went along with the recovery game plan while they were in treatment fully intending to return to chemical use.

And that's not relapse, by the way. Adolescents who return to chemical use the same day they are discharged from treatment have not relapsed; they have just continued to progress in the addictive-progression process. They never entered recovery. This pretreatment stage can last for months or even years before adolescents finally enter recovery. For many, however, this stage can be shortened.

Pretreatment completion is best accomplished on an outpatient basis, in a program which first makes an assessment of adolescents and their families, We need to determine whether or not these adolescents are chemically dependent and also whether anyone else in their family is chemically dependent.

This program should have an outpatient pretreatment group which focuses (1) on connecting consequences to chemical use and (2) on monitoring adolescent control strategies. Pretreatment completion can happen for most chemically dependent adolescents in six to eight weeks. If it doesn't, then it is usually appropriate to structure an intervention on week eight. My experience in using this process has been that most chemically dependent adolescents will *ask* to go to treatment, and that is very exciting.

The major problem with structuring a program that helps adolescents resolve pretreatment issues is that (1) counselors often allow frantic parents to pressure them into placing their adolescents in inpatient treatment prematurely to relieve the family stress; and (2) inpatient treatment centers are concerned that outpatient counselors will keep all their chemically dependent adolescents in outpatient programs.

In our field we have to face the fact that many adolescents don't get sober or stay sober with current treatment practices. Remember the CATOR study shows that 60 to 80 percent of adolescents who have been through treatment resume using chemicals within twelve months. We have to take a pro-active approach in working together to provide treatment programs that work.

The final concern about a pretreatment program is that most of the adolescents are still using chemicals during treatment, and they are encouraged to tell the truth about it. They are *not* encouraged to continue chemical use but they are not forced to lie about their use. Some counselors fear what other people (schools, courts, parents) may think about this. I try to explain to them what pretreatment is about, but I don't compromise the program. My goal is to get as many chemically dependent adolescents as I can into recovery.

Not resolving pretreatment issues *first* forces adolescents into compliance followed by lying and covering up the facts for as long as they can get away with it. Frankly, this is exactly what is happening now. Then when adolescents are caught using again, everyone screams "relapse." Again, no one can be in relapse who has never been in recovery. These adolescents were never sober; they fooled everyone.

Is there ever a time to force adolescents into treatment?

Yes, when they present a threat to themselves or others. For example, adolescents who are suicidal, who have a history of overdosing or have dangerously high chemical use patterns, or who appear homicidal. It is not only appropriate but imperative that these adolescents be hospitalized and safeguarded.

This, however, does not represent the majority of adolescents. Most adolescents will benefit from a pretreatment process that helps them resolve their control issues. Adolescents who resolve pretreatment tasks are motivated to recover, present fewer problems in treatment, move into recovery faster, and have lower relapse rates.

Stabilization

On accepting that they cannot control their use of chemicals, the second stage of recovery for adolescents is stabilization. In this stage they learn how to abstain. The **stabilization tasks of the ADMR** are to (1) recover from acute and post-acute withdrawal; (2) stabilize from their motivational crisis; (3) accept the need for help; (4) interrupt addictive preoccupation; (5) recognize the possibility of an alternative life-style; (6) learn nonchemical stress management; and (7) develop hope and motivation.

Recovery from acute withdrawal is detoxification which should be medically managed if the child has used chemicals in the past seventy-two hours or if he or she displays symptoms of physical withdrawal. Stabilization of post-acute withdrawal (PAW) symptoms is the next step.

PAW was identified by Terence Gorski as a bio-psycho-social phenomenon in recovering people which results from brain damage. PAW emerges following detoxification and is a physical, psychological, and social reaction to abstinence. When chemically dependent adolescents decide to give up chemical use they will have psychological issues around loss, grief, and anxiety about the decision. Socially, they will experience fear, confusion, and frustration. Physically, they will usually have symptoms such as headaches and stomachaches, among others.

Other symptoms of PAW include difficulty in thinking clearly, in numbering things, in focusing attention, and in following a logical sequence of events. Rigid, repetitive thoughts emerge, and there is difficulty in managing feelings and emotions. There is a tendency to overreact to situations or not be able to feel anything at all, to be "numbed off." There is difficulty managing even low levels of stress. Adolescents often experience sleep disturbances: They are not able to fall asleep or to remain asleep or they are awakened by disturbing or bad dreams. This sleep interruption can last for days or weeks or be intermittent, with periods of long sleep.

PAW symptoms emerge following detoxification and return during periods of stress. Teaching recovering adolescents about PAW helps to relieve the stress associated with experiencing it. It is common for them to believe these symptoms mean they are going crazy. In addition to education, it is necessary to teach them management strategies for coping with the PAW symptoms they experience. Without effective management strategies, they will often return to chemicals to medicate these symptoms.

Adolescents need to **stabilize from their motivational crisis;** the situation or events that served to break through their denial about their chemical use are usually traumatic for them. Next, chemically dependent adolescents have to **accept the need for help.** Once they recognize in pretreatment that they cannot control their chemical use, they need to understand that recovery is a process that will require guidance and support. Pointing out that they are a failure at staying sober *without help* should be clarified. This leads to getting them involved with other recovering people with whom they can begin to bond and helps them let go of the notion that they can do this alone.

Interrupting addictive preoccupation means assisting the chemically dependent adolescent to pull out of repetitive thoughts about procuring the drug, using the drug, and recovering from the effects of the drug. It involves teaching adolescents to stop reminiscing about drug-related incidents (telling war stories) and shifting their focus of attention to ways of changing this behavior.

Adolescents have to believe that there is "life after drugs." They have to *recognize that an alternative life-style is possible.* Most chemically dependent adolescents have no idea how to relax, have fun, cope with problems, or how to use leisure time without chemicals. Therefore, introducing them to recovering adolescents who have been successful in a Twelve-Step program is necessary. Chemically dependent adolescents need real-life examples to gain a vision of what is possible.

Learning nonchemical stress management means figuring out how to cope with painful or stressful situations without chemicals. Adolescents can be taught alternatives to managing stress, such as relaxation exercises, physical activity, pursuing hobbies, and talking with others to process feelings.

Finally, adolescents need to *develop hope and motivation:* hope that recovery for them is possible and the motivation to go after it. Again, if it is possible, the best way to do this is to have them see what other recovering adolescents are doing. They can begin to recognize the possibility and the benefits of an alternative life-style by going into the recovering community and finding solidly recovering young people. Recovering adolescents are usually very willing to volunteer to help their newly abstinent peers who are just trying to stabilize.

Adolescents need to see that people who are recovering

aren't living miserable, aimless, boring lives. They don't know that there is an alternative to what they are doing, and they have to be shown that there is. They can't be motivated without live evidence. They want to believe that it is possible for adolescents to recover and actually enjoy it. They can start by visiting a young AA or NA group.

In this stage of recovery, the adolescent learns how to become *comfortably* abstinent. In the past, the adolescent has depended on chemicals as mood elevators, to help cope with stress, frustration, anger and other problems, and as a way to have fun. Now they have to learn how to function on a minute-by-minute, hour-by-hour, and day-by-day basis that doesn't include chemicals.

Early Recovery

The **early recovery tasks of the ADMR** are (1) to establish an externally regulated recovery program; (2) to recognize the nature and presence of their addictive disease; (3) to accept and integrate knowledge of their addiction; (4) to learn appropriate impulse control and deferred gratification; (5) to develop a sobriety-centered value system; and (6) to learn to cope with family dynamics.

Establishing an externally regulated recovery program means that it will be necessary for a professional to outline a recovery program of activities because the adolescent lacks knowledge of how to live a meaningful life sober. **Recognizing the nature of addictive disease** involves gaining understanding that this will not go away, that if untreated it gets worse, and that it is prone to relapse. **Accepting their addiction** means learning to deal with their guilt, shame, and remorse about being chemically dependent.

Learning impulse control and delayed gratification is difficult for chemically dependent people—more so for chemically dependent adolescents who are struggling with the concept of time (see chapter 3 entitled "Normal Adolescent Development.") Learning to wait, think, and plan are all things we have to teach these adolescents, or they will drink or drug now and think about it later. The younger the adolescent, the more challenging this task will be.

Developing a sobriety-centered value system means shifting from a chemical-centered value system (procurring drugs, using drugs, and recovering from the effects of drugs) to a way of life that has meaning and fulfillment and that is sober. This is best accomplished by associating with people who have done it.

Early recovery involves developing a foundation of abstinence that is solid. This is when young people should be introduced to a Twelve-Step program such as Alcoholics Anonymous, Narcotics Anonymous, Cocaine Anonymous, or whichever support group is appropriate for them. This is where they find out that "in order to learn how to live sober and *like* it, I'm going to have to hang around folks who have done it and can help me do it." This is also where adolescents develop the spiritual part of the recovery program, and that is accomplished by getting them started in working the Twelve-Step program that has helped so many chemically dependent people stay sober.

The final task in early recovery is *learning to cope with current family dynamics.* We do not encourage adults to explore their family-of-origin issues in early recovery because it often throws them into relapse. Adolescents don't really have a choice—first, because they have to go back to their families and live there; second, because they have not locked on to their roles and to family beliefs as hard as someone who is forty or fifty years old. Forty- or fifty-year-olds have locked on to a belief system and centered their lives around it. It is often shattering to them to find they've lived a lie for forty or more years.

It is possible to sit down with an adolescent who comes from a dysfunctional or alcoholic family and talk about this. You can explain some of the family's patterns: the unwritten rules, the family secrets, the roles everybody has in the family, the adolescent's role in this system. When you say, "This isn't a healthy system," the adolescent will say, "Yeah, I guess it isn't." When you say that to adults who have operated forty years of their lives—based their careers, their ambitions, all their relationships—around mistaken beliefs, they find it difficult to accept.

In learning to cope with current family dynamics, adolescents need first to identify the primary thinking, emotional, and behavior patterns they learned as young children. They need to look at their perception of themselves and the world that they developed as a result of being in their family.

Next, they identify the belief structures that support those patterns. They come to understand why they operate the way they do and what they understood their family messages to be regarding what was expected of them. Then they have to judge these beliefs and decide, "Which of these is good for me or bad for me? Which of these beliefs do I want to hold on to?"

For example, one of my clients, a forty-year-old woman named Edith, learned as a child that "people who work hard to please authority figures are rewarded for it," and "the harder you work, the better you will be rewarded." Her family supported that idea by rewarding Edith's "good" hardworking behaviors. When she was very young, her mother would bake cookies or give her other "goodies" for doing certain things and for her accomplishments. She received rewards for the successes she had then.

When Edith got a little older, the "goodies" got a little more expensive. Then it would be a new bike or a dress. In those preadolescent years, her family could afford to see that she was rewarded for overachievement. The problem was, she left home as an adult still believing that was the way the world operated. She believed that people who work hard, sacrifice, put in more, and give more always get more.

When Edith was approaching her fortieth birthday, she looked around one day and said, "Wait a minute! What am I getting for all the effort I've put forth and the sacrifices I've made?" She had spent years in college living with her nose in a book. After college she went through special training. She developed programs and did what she called "trench work." She'd been out getting experience and doing difficult jobs just so she could say she'd "been there" and had been sacrificing everything else, literally. Edith had sacrificed financially and in every other way. In terms of a social life, she'd given it all up. Why? Because she believed she would get "something good" for this. And at the age of forty the "something good" still wasn't happening.

One day Edith said, "What's going on here? I'm not rich. As a matter of fact, I'm not making as much as a lot of the people right here working around me. And I'm not famous. And nobody's running around giving me any 'atta girls.'" At that time, this was a crisis for her. Finally, she said, "Look, something's got to give here!"

So Edith decided that the premise that "the work ethic is rewarded" was a mistaken belief she had accepted from her parents. The truth is, hard work is not always rewarded. Edith realized that there were many people who worked even harder, sacrificed more, and did not even get as much as she did in return. She had to decide: "Do I walk around with this chip on my shoulder about the fact that I put in a lot more and I'm not getting anything out? Or do I get rid of it now and recognize that the bill of goods [mistaken beliefs] my family sold me isn't borne out in the real world?" This was simply a bill of goods sold to her parents that they had never challenged.

Edith decided to rid herself of this idea, but it wasn't easy.

She had to really do some work on herself to overcome her belief that if she sacrificed now she would reap benefits later. I think she's recovering, except that she told me she experiences relapses occasionally. Sometimes when her nephew performs well, she still runs to the cookie jar.

That's how adolescents need to work through this part of early recovery. With each of the behaviors that they're acting out, adolescents need to explore what belief is behind it and where they learned it. They need to find out what their perception of that belief is and how it determines their role to achieve, to fail, to avoid—whatever it is—and whether or not they want to change that. They need to challenge what they have been taught to believe to determine if it is valid for them in the real world.

Middle Recovery

In this stage adolescents develop an age-appropriate balanced life-style which means learning to function well in all aspects of their lives. AA calls it "practicing these principles in all our affairs." Adolescents need to take the principles they have learned through their recovery from chemical dependency into their school, work, and home environment.

The **middle recovery tasks of the ADMR are** (1) to develop healthy self-esteem; (2) to clarify personal values; (3) to learn to recognize healthy personal preferences; (4) to repair addiction-caused social damage; and (5) to establish a self-regulated recovery program.

The first thing adolescents need to do in this stage is to *develop healthy self-esteem.* That's not easy for any adolescent, and it is especially difficult for chemically dependent adolescents who have the added stigma and self-concept that they are basically "bad" persons because of their addictive disease.

We've all heard folks say things like, "She didn't have a

chance; she's got 'bad blood,' " or "She came out of a bad family," as if the person has no chance or choice. Some adolescents have to deal with this. They have to understand that just because they are genetically predisposed to chemical dependence doesn't mean they do not have a choice or a chance. It doesn't mean they were born with "bad blood."

The other piece of this is that even if you start to help these adolescents and they start responding to treatment, they often find that the rest of the world doesn't believe they are trying to recover. People often continue to treat these adolescents in the same way they did when the adolescents were using chemicals; some people want to keep them in "bad boy" or "bad girl" roles. Many adolescents work hard in recovery, yet their parents, schoolteachers, and peers fail to accept the fact that they really are trying to change.

The task of **clarifying personal values** ties in to the normal adolescent development process as well. They must decide, "What is it that I believe in? What's important to me? What's right? What's wrong? What's good for me? What's bad for me? What's best for the 'common good' of all?" Adolescents start to gain insight regarding what they believe with sober, clear minds.

It is the same in **learning to recognize healthy personal preferences.** Adolescents need to find out what is in their best interest and what isn't. They need to learn to recognize what works best for them and what doesn't—how they would like their lives to be, including friends, hobbies, etc.

Adolescents need to *repair their addiction-caused social damage.* In Twelve-Step programs this is addressed through working Steps Eight and Nine, and "making amends to those they have harmed." They must work on damaged relationships with parents and friends. Recovering adolescents also need to develop appropriate social skills. Many times they don't know how to relate to other adolescents who aren't "into drugs." They don't know how to have a conversation with what they call a "normy," a normal adolescent. They don't know how to interact with folks who aren't or weren't part of the drug subculture.

Role-playing social situations can help adolescents learn these skills. First they practice in their therapy groups. Then they go out and practice with one other person and come back and report on how that went. They get support from their groups to help them pick up the pieces and try again when not everybody responds positively to them or to the changes they are trying to make.

At this point, adolescents should be *establishing self-regulated recovery programs.* They should be telling you what they need and what they think will work best for them. They should be saying things like, "Okay, look. I still want to do group about twice a week. But I don't think I still need four AA meetings a week, so I'm dropping that down to two. And I probably really need to see my counselor one-on-one just once a month, but I'd like to have something regular set up so I can spend a little more time working with my dad on some of our issues."

Eventually this happens with recovering adolescents, and when it does, they are right on course. They still need counseling but only for a little guidance. If they are going to stay sober for the rest of their lives, they must reach the point that they recognize what their needs are and outline their own recovery programs.

Late Recovery

In the late recovery stage, adolescents establish the healthy interdependence with others they need in order to function in the world. They come to understand that "no man is an island" and that they need other people to maintain their sobriety. They realize that they are going to have to live and work cooperatively with others.

The **late recovery tasks of the ADMR** are (1) to develop

intimacy skills; (2) to adopt a cooperative attitude toward society; (3) to learn to appropriately self-assess; and (4) to develop independent action and thought.

In late recovery, adolescents start to work on **developing intimacy skills.** One of the things that many adolescents in Twelve-Step programs hear often is that they shouldn't get into relationships for a while after entering recovery, meaning relationships with the opposite sex. The reasons are that (1) most chemically dependent people don't know what healthy relationships are, and (2) these relationships interfere with their ability to focus on their recovery tasks.

We can endorse this concept, but the reality is that most adolescents will not comply. We have to accept the fact that these adolescents are entering relationships. We need to help them determine whether or not the characteristics of their relationships are healthy. They need to learn to recognize whether or not the interpersonal relationships that they are developing are meeting their needs and requirements for a partner.

Adolescents' struggles with this provide opportunities to start talking with them about what healthy relationships are. Many of them didn't see any while they were growing up, and now they have the opportunity to start learning. Sadly, there's usually no training for the most important events in our lives such as getting married and having children. These are subjects we can talk about in therapy that will be very helpful to these adolescents. Many of them have not had positive role models and don't have a solid base on which to start.

Recovering chemically dependent adolescents need to **adopt a cooperative attitude toward society.** Note that this is also the last stage of the **individuation, separation, autonomy, and cooperation development process** for normal adolescents. In learning cooperation adolescents recognize that they're going to have to interact with other folks in order to stay sober as well as to be successful in other areas of their lives.

They can say, "I'm going to have to get along with you, even though I don't like you, because you're my boss and I need the paycheck. I'm going to have to get along with this guy, because I want to go to college, and he's interviewing me for the job I need. I think he's a jerk, but I'm not going to let him know it. I'm going to play this game with him anyway." Adolescents need to learn they have to get along with people to get their needs met.

Adolescents need to *learn to appropriately assess themselves;* to be able to say to themselves, "These are my strengths and weaknesses. This is what I like about myself and these are the things I have to work on that I'm not proud of." Adolescents also need to *develop independent action and thought,* which is the final stage of adolescence. This means being able to make decisions for themselves in the world they live in, based on running things through their own brains, their own level of knowledge, and their own life experiences.

Some of us find it difficult to help adolescents through their developmental issues because they bring us to places where we are stuck in our own development. Many of us either have unresolved adolescent issues of our own or had such a hard time resolving them that they're still matters that are difficult for us. When we encounter a child in a therapeutic relationship who is working on some of those same issues, we often find somebody who can really "push our buttons."

In trying to help adolescents through recovery, if we are also in recovery ourselves, we cannot take a child further than we are in the process. When an adolescent with whom we are working gets to us, we need to try to identify why this is happening. We may find that these adolescents have some personality issues similar to our own. Or they may represent persons who gave us a hard time when we were struggling

143

with similar problems. We may be surprised how much they bring to us that is a reflection of our own issues.

Maintenance

In the maintenance stage adolescents continue their growth and development. The mainstay for this is lifelong participation in AA/NA, plus relapse prevention planning because they are always at risk for relapse.

The maintenance tasks of the ADMR are (1) to maintain a recovery program; (2) to maintain effective day-to-day coping skills; (3) to maintain continued growth and development; (4) to follow productive life planning; and (5) to learn to cope effectively with life transitions and complicating factors.

Maintaining a recovery program means never losing sight of recovery as a primary goal. It also means remembering that all life decisions must take into account the need to continue to work a recovery program.

Maintaining effective day-to-day coping skills is essential. Allowing problems to accumulate without taking action places adolescents at risk of feeling overwhelmed, and feeling overwhelmed increases their risk of relapse. **Continued personal growth** means completing adolescent development tasks. Participating in **productive life planning** consists of making future plans, setting goals, and working toward achieving these goals. **Learning to cope with life transitions as well as complicating factors** means learning to accept circumstances or life problems that can't be changed and making the best of these situations.

A recovering adolescent's chemical addiction is something that does not go away. Once people are chemically dependent, they are always chemically dependent. They are either actively chemically dependent or inactively chemically dependent; they are either in recovery or they are experiencing relapse.

Recovery is a process, not an event, just as grief is the process when death is the event. Trying to recover from chemicals is like running up a "down" escalator, if you can visualize that. If you run hard enough and really exert yourself, you can gain momentum against that moving escalator and actually make progress upward. But what happens when you stand still? The escalator brings you right back down. That's what happens when people stand still in the recovery process.

Once adolescents have actually entered recovery they are at all times either in the process of recovery or in the process of relapse.

People in recovery from chemical addiction have to work hard against the odds to make progressive movement up the "wellness escalator." When they get stuck in their recovery programs because they don't know what to do or they just get lazy, they move into the relapse process. Relapse is something that faces all chemically dependent people; it can become a problem for them at any time for the rest of their lives.

Once adolescents have actually entered recovery they are at all times either in the process of recovery or in the process of relapse; they are never just standing still. They are either actively pursuing recovery or they are actively sliding into relapse.

Chapter
7

Adolescent Relapse Warning Signs

Relapse does not simply mean a return to chemical use. Just like recovery, relapse is also a process. It is a process that progresses over time and ends in chemical use. The definition of relapse is, "the process of becoming dysfunctional in sobriety that often ends in chemical use" (Terence T. Gorski).

In AA this is called "a dry drunk." It is also called BUD (Building Up to Drink). As the relapse process progresses, it can become so uncomfortable that the adolescent feels that using alcohol or drugs can't be any worse than the pain of trying to stay sober.

The relapse process was identified as a syndrome (a collection of predictable symptoms that precede chemical use) by Gorski (1973). Relapse warning signs for adults were originally published by CENAPS in 1980 and have been revised several times since.

I began using these relapse warning signs with adolescents in 1982. I noticed that recovering adolescents had different warning signs than recovering adults. They responded better to relapse prevention therapy when the warning signs were written to address their specific experiences.

For adolescents, relapse means they are abstinent, they

are working a recovery program, and then their lives start to go out of control again. When they are dysfunctional, they are in the relapse dynamic.

Because the relapse process ends in chemical use, it is not helpful to define relapse as simply a return to chemical use. To do so limits our ability to diagnose and to intervene on the symptoms that precede a relapse to chemical use.

For adolescents, relapse means they are abstinent, they are working a recovery program, and then their lives start to go out of control again.

Relapse doesn't have to be the end of the world. Adolescents can get back into recovery, particularly if they have been taught about relapse. The majority of chemically dependent people have experienced relapse during their recovery even though many have never experienced it to the point that they returned to chemicals again. Any time recovering persons become dysfunctional in sobriety, particularly while under high stress, they may enter the relapse process.

It is important to educate adolescents to the fact that this disease is prone to relapse, that most of them are going to experience relapse, and that some of them are going to relapse all the way back to chemical use. Telling adolescents this is not in any way giving them "permission" to relapse. We are *not* telling them, "You can't help relapsing; it's part of the disease." We are defining the disease for them. Besides, they have never needed our permission to relapse before, have they?

By telling adolescents this we give many of them permission to come back into recovery. If they believe that relapse

148

means they are personal failures, they won't come back. When I first came into this field it was common to blame the patient when relapse occurred. We didn't see at the time that there was a great deal about addiction that we didn't understand. Now we know that people go into relapse for many reasons, one of them being that we don't have all the answers about chemical addiction.

Adolescents are all-or-nothing thinkers, and they see themselves as successful or as failures: there is nothing in between. We have to educate them right from the start that that's not what recovery is at all. The recovery process does not unfold in a matter of weeks. It takes a long time for anyone, and particularly for adolescents.

We have to make sure that adolescents continue in therapy, as well as Twelve-Step programs. This means one to two years of professional counseling for chemically dependent adolescents.

Granted, the second year of therapy is not as intense as it is in the first year. By the second year of recovery adolescents are still involved in sobriety groups which meet regularly, plus they attend AA or NA—which they are going to do the rest of their lives. The professional therapy piece needs to be in place for nothing short of one to two years to reduce relapse. Adolescents need to connect with somebody who can provide long-term recovery and relapse prevention planning.

There are adolescents who can work this entire model on an outpatient basis. These adolescents are those who (1) can abstain; (2) come from at least a fairly functional family; and (3) are not suffering from an unmanageable dual diagnosis.

For adolescents who cannot work effectively with an outpatient program there is a second level of treatment where they can be detoxified and stabilized, and then placed into a structured intensive outpatient program. This is not just once-a-week individual or group counseling session. It is a structured, *intensive* outpatient program.

Intensive outpatient therapy typically involves a minimum of four hours of therapy, education, or recovery-centered activities at least four nights a week, plus attendance at three or more Twelve-Step meetings weekly. In addition, sobriety-centered social activities and family therapy are provided. Preferably, this level of therapy is available for ten to twelve weeks and no less than six weeks. The second phase of intensive outpatient treatment centers around sobriety groups meeting twice a week, plus continued attendance at Twelve-Step meetings and family therapy for twelve to eighteen months.

Relapse doesn't have to be the end of the world.

The third level of treatment is for the adolescent who cannot abstain, has a dual or multiple diagnosis, comes from a severely dysfunctional family, or is a threat to himself or society. If any of these problems are present, adolescents will need to go inpatient to work on their recovery initially, followed by long-term intensive outpatient therapy—not the aftercare programs where the adolescent comes back for six weeks for a once-a-week group. Once-a-week programs are simply inadequate for adolescents. This is one reason why relapse is so high for this age-group. They need outpatient *therapy* or a "halfway house," not just outpatient aftercare, following their discharge from inpatient treatment.

Why People Relapse

The major reason for relapse is that chemical dependency is a disease that is prone to relapse. It is not just adolescents who relapse; so do a large number of adults. In fact, 40 to 60 percent of recovering chemically dependent people relapse at least once following their first serious attempts at treatment (Gorski, 1982). It is not uncommon for recovering persons to find themselves dysfunctional and entertaining the thought of chemical use. It is part of the nature of the disease of addiction that relapse will be a problem for many people.

Why Adolescents Relapse

Recovering adolescents are at higher risk of relapse because they are in a stage of growth which involves many physical and emotional changes. Many adolescents relapse due to these normal adolescent growth issues. Their chemical dependency has delayed their normal development, making it difficult for recovering chemically dependent adolescents to function the way they should for their age. This causes them to be very uncomfortable, sometimes to the point of being dysfunctional in the way they think, feel, and behave. Some adolescents return to using chemicals to medicate this discomfort. Recovering adolescents and their care givers need to be able to recognize the physical, emotional, and behavioral warning signs that indicate the young person has entered the relapse process.

There are some **predisposing factors** that can cause adolescents to get stuck in their recovery or to start the relapse cycle. Predisposed simply means "something that puts you at high risk for" or "something that makes you an 'easy mark.'" For example, if chemical dependency is in your family, you are predisposed to chemical dependency.

Predisposing factors to relapse for adolescents include learning disabilities, dual or multiple diagnosis, having a high stress personality (the Type A person), inadequate coping skills, lack of a support system, dysfunctional families, and lack of impulse control. The risk of relapse will be higher for adolescents who enter recovery with one or more of these problems. Many of these predisposing factors can be diagnosed, addressed, and treated. There is no need for these factors to present a surprise when they start to interfere with an adolescent's recovery.

Besides predisposing factors, there are also **precipitating factors.** These are happenings that upset adolescents and their ability to work a recovery program, such as a situational crisis or a major life change. A big one for adolescents is when parents divorce or separate—if Dad or Mom leaves.

Another is emotional loss from such occurrences as moving away from old friends, changing schools, or the loss or death of a family member. For a teenager, perhaps the biggest emotional loss is breaking up with a girl friend or boyfriend. These are painful things they can't plan for specifically but that can be expected to add to the possibility of relapse.

The important thing for adolescents, their families, and counselors to learn is that they can intervene on the relapse process and possibly prevent a return to chemical use.

The important thing for adolescents, their families, and counselors to learn is that they can intervene on the relapse process and possibly prevent a return to chemical use by recognizing the relapse warning signs.

Relapse warning signs are physical symptoms, emotional responses, and behaviors that are present prior to the adolescent's picking up a drink or a drug. There is a natural progression of internal and external symptoms of dysfunction when most adolescents get more and more uncomfortable, they decide that life is just as bad sober as it was when they were using chemicals. They start to think, "I might as well be using so I won't have to deal with this."

It is important that adolescents are able to recognize these relapse warning signs early in recovery. It is common for them to experience some of these symptoms from time to time throughout the recovery process. If adolescents are aware of what is happening, they can take steps to interrupt the relapse process when they or those close to them see these warning signs of relapse. But they need to know what the symptoms are.

Adolescent Relapse Warning Signs
PHASE ONE
Return of Denial

Return of denial starts when a recovering adolescent begins to feel frustrated and confused around people and in certain situations. Some of the most common symptoms that bring about the return of denial are difficulty in thinking clearly, managing feelings and emotions, remembering things, managing stress, and sleeping restfully; problems with physical coordination and accidents; and feelings of being defective or even "crazy."

Denial of these symptoms is a natural response to the fear, guilt, and shame adolescents may feel if they believe that these symptoms mean they are doing something wrong in their recovery. The warning signs of return of denial can be subtle and deceptive as they are often **normal** behaviors for nonrecovering adolescents.

Warning Sign No. 1: Impatience and frustration. Adolescents become impatient with parents who still do not trust them and with teachers who still treat them as a "bad adolescent." They become frustrated with a world which doesn't seem to give them recognition or immediate forgiveness following their recent treatment accomplishments. They think, "No one trusts me or believes me. Things have not changed at all!"

Impatience with people and situations and frequent frustration are not signs of quality sobriety. They are easy to dismiss once in a while; we all have some bad days. But if this is happening regularly, then it may be that the adolescent is becoming dysfunctional—meaning having difficulty in thinking clearly or in managing his or her feelings, emotions, and behavior—and in denial about these early relapse warning signs.

Warning Sign No. 2: "Everything-is-OK." Once in recovery, most chemically dependent adolescents talk honestly about their thoughts and feelings every day. When they begin to experience frustration in their recovery programs, they try to back off from others so they don't have to engage or interact on any deep or meaningful level.

They develop the "everything-is-OK" syndrome. When they are told that the quality of their participation in group and in individual sessions is going down, that it is not the meaningful contribution it used to be, their responses may be vague. Adolescents will say, "Don't worry about it, I'm fine." When confronted, they will say, "Nothing's wrong."

PHASE TWO
Avoidance and Defensive Behavior

Phase Two is referred to in AA/NA as "white knuckle sobriety." In this phase, adolescents' behaviors and attitudes begin to change and their discomfort becomes visible to observant parents or counselors. Signs of Phase Two include such attitudes and behaviors as the following:

Warning Sign No. 3: Believing "I'll never drink/use again." Because of their denial, adolescents pretend to feel

154

good (or they feel numb). They are not aware of their problems or feelings. They convince themselves that they will never use alcohol or drugs again. When they firmly believe that they "have it made," the need to work a daily recovery program loses importance. Sometimes they tell this to others, but usually they keep it to themselves due to fear of what others would say. A small part of them knows that something is wrong but they refuse to think or talk about it.

Warning Sign No. 4: Worrying about others instead of self. As adolescents become convinced that they have "good" programs and will never use alcohol or drugs again, they begin doing what people in AA/NA call "working the other person's program." In therapy (aftercare) groups and Twelve-Step meetings, these adolescents become actively involved with the recovery of others but stop talking about their own problems. In group therapy they behave as if they are role models of recovery and attempt to counsel other adolescents.

Warning Sign No. 5: Resentment toward drinkers and users. Adolescents develop strong resentments toward drinkers and users. They start to judge, criticize, put down, and really take a hard-line approach to other people who are using chemicals, including social drinkers. This resentment grows from their being angry that others can drink when they can't rather than accepting their disease.

They begin to analyze the drinking or drug behavior of family and friends and point out that these behavior patterns are consistent with addiction. They may become verbally abusive toward family members and friends who drink and condemn past associates for their continued use.

Warning Sign No. 6: Beginning to avoid family gatherings. Though not in total isolation, adolescents will begin falling back from the family again. They may want to take their dinner to their room or try to limit conversations with Mom and Dad. They may not want to go places with family members, even to those places that they formerly liked to go.

Warning Sign No. 7: Dwelling on treatment experience. When adolescents come out of treatment, particularly inpatient programs, and start into ongoing outpatient therapy (aftercare), they may begin to reminisce about how wonderful inpatient was. Life is no longer centered around them, as it was there, but their desire for that kind of attention is still strong.

This is a sign that adolescents are having difficulty coping with stress and sober life. They didn't have to cope with the real world in treatment. Now they are required to cope with teachers, bosses, parents, sisters, brothers, and friends.

They didn't have to cope with the real world in treatment. Now they are required to cope with teachers, bosses, parents, sisters, brothers, and friends.

Adolescents will start to reminisce about how everybody cared about and loved them in treatment, and how everybody hugged each other there. Deep down inside they know that is not the real world. The subtle message they're trying to give others is, "I'm not being listened to. I'm not being understood. Things are going wrong in my recovery and nobody's paying any attention."

Warning Sign No. 8: Superficial aftercare involvement. Even though adolescents are still going to aftercare, they now take more passive roles. They don't have the real motivation that they had at first; that real lock-on "give me more" kind of recovery attitude is gone. They stop bringing legitimate (recovery) problems to group to work on. Their discussion is focused on complaining about their parents, their AA/NA sponsor, or school. Eventually, they start to miss group more often.

PHASE THREE
Crisis Building

In Phase Three, relapsing adolescents begin to demonstrate problems with thinking. They can't think straight sometimes and they even start thinking secretly that they are going "crazy."

Warning Sign No. 9: Concentration and memory problems. Adolescents may have problems concentrating on school assignments, forget assignments, and have problems getting started in the morning. They will say, "I got a 'D' on a test that I *studied* for! I can do *that* well without studying. But I studied for this one and it was all I could do to remember how to put my name on the paper!"

Warning Sign No. 10: Rigid, impaired, or inappropriate judgment. Adolescents become unwilling to receive and process input different from their own point of view. This is especially noticeable in group meetings where they have a need to be right and to convince others to believe the same way they do. They lock onto one thing and are not able to see anything outside of it.

At times adolescents may be *too* "open and honest." They may "tell it like it is" to people who can't handle this. Often this may result in consequences that can lead to serious problems.

Warning Sign No. 11: Procrastination. Adolescents are slow to begin school assignments and they stop progressing in their AA/NA Step work. They start using excuses such as, "I'm not ready to work on that Step yet."

Warning Sign No. 12: Believing that people expect too much. When confronted about the presence of relapse behaviors, adolescents become angry and defensive. They feel that other people's expectations of them are unrealistic and will ask, "What do they want from me? I went to that program. I'm not doing drugs. I'm going to meetings. I have a sponsor. Now I have to be nice and happy all the time too? I don't know what people want from me."

Warning Sign No. 13: Misuse of recovery principles. Adolescents begin to misinterpret recovery principles to justify their current problems in recovery. For example, they mistakenly believe that "rigorous honesty" gives them the right to insult and criticize others; that "one day at a time" means don't plan for tomorrow; "easy does it" means it's OK not to do anything that they don't want to do; "turn it over" means they are not responsible for anything; and "stick with the winners" means that no one else in a recovery program is good enough to help them.

Warning Sign No. 14: Strained relationships with family. Lack of trust develops between adolescents and their parents. Adolescents may analyze and challenge their parents' motives for admitting them to treatment. Because they now understand chemical dependency and related disorders, adolescents think they can evaluate others as having these problems as well. Their parents start to think, "Oh, boy! Now we have an obnoxious, amateur psychologist on our hands!" As things like this start to happen, relationships within the adolescent's family begin to be strained.

PHASE FOUR
Immobilization

In Phase Four, relapsing adolescents return to escape tactics for relief. They lose the ability to control their attitudes, behavior, and moods. They say, "If only I didn't have to go to AA, if I had different parents, or if I could just go live in another town, then my life would be better."

Warning Sign No. 15: Daydreaming and "spacing out." Adolescents escape from the "real world" by engaging in fantasies which create the world as they would like it to be. They are caught staring off into space during activities such as family events, group sessions, or private conversations. In group therapy and individual sessions they "space out"—the lights are on but "nobody's home."

Warning Sign No. 16: Unpredictable mood swings. Adolescents' moods and behaviors vary from day to day, or from one extreme to the other within the same day. No one knows what moods or behaviors to expect from them because they react differently to similar situations.

Warning Sign No. 17: Problems at school reappear. Adolescents' grades begin to fall and their teachers resume complaints about their behavior. They are late for school or cut classes altogether. They start to lose control of their lives while abstinent, and, although they're still attempting to work a recovery program, they are clearly in the process of relapse.

PHASE FIVE
Confusion and Overreaction

In Phase Five, relapsing adolescents begin to have problems caused by neglecting their recovery programs. During this phase they experience internal anguish, which is much more severe than the discomfort they felt in the earlier phases. They begin to lose faith in the treatment system.

Warning Sign No. 18: Periods of confusion. Adolescents begin to have periods of confusion that become more frequent, last longer, and cause more problems. They feel angry with themselves because they can't seem to figure things out. They start to believe they must be either dumb or crazy.

Warning Sign No. 19: Home-life problems intensify. Adolescents may find that their entire family is relapsing along with them. It may seem that everyone is becoming angry at home. As high levels of stress return, their family becomes dysfunctional again.

Warning Sign No. 20: Loss of confidence in AA/NA friends and counselors. Relapsing adolescents start to renounce AA/NA traditions and aftercare and attempt to "work the program" in their own way. They see no significance in missing group or meetings.

They start evaluating and taking other people's inventories, and they are critical of people in AA/NA and put personalities before principles. They say, "I don't like that meeting because there's too many old people in it" (usually meaning people over thirty). "I don't like this meeting because there's a woman who tells the same dumb story over and over again." Or, "I'm going to fire my sponsor. I don't like him anymore." They start to pull away from the professionals who are there to help them and from their peers in recovery as well.

As these relationships become strained, adolescents feel threatened if other people mention noticing changes in their behavior and moods. Conflicts continue to increase in spite of their efforts to resolve them. Adolescents begin to feel guilty and remorseful about their role in these conflicts.

Warning Sign No. 21: Overreacting to real or imag-

ined criticism. Relapsing adolescents do not react favorably to any form of criticism, even from their peer support. They take suggestions as insults and begin to personalize everything that is said to them as a direct threat or attack.

Warning Sign No. 22: Recovering peers start to complain. Adolescents who are in aftercare or outpatient programs find that their group members are confronting them. Anger and frustration develop in their group. As trust and communication break down, efforts to eliminate them from the group begin. The other group members complain to the counselor that the adolescent's attitude and behavior are disruptive. They say, "Get him out of our group. He's ruining our group. We don't want him in here anymore."

PHASE SIX
Depression

Relapsing adolescents become aware of the impairments in all areas of their lives—physical, mental, and emotional. They become so depressed that they have difficulty keeping normal routines. By this phase their family and peers have become frustrated.

Warning Sign No. 23: Experiencing boredom and apathy. Adolescents no longer find stimulation in AA/NA meetings, in aftercare, or in school. They say, "I'm bored." "I don't have anything to do." The old "I don't care" attitude returns.

Warning Sign No. 24: Becoming edgy and irritable. Relapsing adolescents "jump all over" anyone who questions them or makes the slightest comment of concern. Family members, friends, and sometimes even counselors find themselves tiptoeing around to avoid hearing these adolescents' harsh words and sarcastic remarks.

Warning Sign No. 25: Becoming lazy and uncoopera-tive. Adolescents spend more of their time sleeping. They may be sleeping in school and refuse to do their household chores and school assignments.

Warning Sign No. 26: Periods of deep depression. Adolescents feel depressed more often. The depression becomes worse, lasts longer, and interferes with living. It becomes so bad that it is noticed by others and cannot be easily denied. Their depression is most severe during unplanned or unstructured periods. When these adolescents feel depressed, they isolate or become irritable and angry with others, and complain that nobody cares or understands what they are going through.

Warning Sign No. 27: Health and physical appearance declines. In early recovery, adolescents start to take a great deal of interest in how they look and what they wear and to care about their health. They resumed the normal adolescent tasks of becoming self-conscious about their appearance. Now in relapse, their pride of self starts to go away again.

They abandon the life-style changes they learned in treatment and their poor eating and sleeping habits return. They may have a loss or gain in weight. They look tired and no longer have that healthy look in their eyes that they had on completing inpatient treatment.

Warning Sign No. 28: Returning to chemical-using associates. Adolescents feel misunderstood by their family and by other recovering people. They are now completely isolated, internally dysfunctional, in trouble at home and at school again, and yet they're still not using alcohol or drugs. They turn to former chemical-using associates, but only for companionship.

They begin to entertain the idea that "I can go back to my old friends, but not to drink or use drugs. I'm *not* going to use." And they mean it. At this point the adolescent has no intention of using.

They say, "I'm going to go back to my old friends because I can relate to those guys." While they were under the influence of chemicals, they believed mistakenly that they were really relating to these people. They say, "We got real."

Warning Sign No. 29: Believing sobriety is miserable. To relapsing adolescents, things seem so bad in sobriety that they begin to think that they might as well be using alcohol or drugs. They think, "Things couldn't possibly get worse, and at least then I could feel good for a little while."

Life seems to be just as unmanageable as it was before they stopped drinking and using. They begin to think, "If this is sobriety, who needs it?" They feel powerless and helpless. They begin to believe that there is no way out and nothing that they can do will correct the problems they are having.

PHASE SEVEN
Behavioral Loss of Control

Adolescents experience progressive and disabling loss of behavioral control that begins to cause serious problems for them with school, work, friends, and relatives. Support from their families is rapidly deteriorating. Their parents usually begin complaining to them during this phase, if they haven't before. Parents usually accuse their adolescents of drinking or using and openly share their feelings of anger, frustration, and resentment.

Warning Sign No. 30: Using improbable excuses for behaviors. Adolescents turn to dishonesty and manipulation to defend and justify their behavior or lack of progress. The stories they design to cover their relapse symptoms become pretty unbelievable. When people question them further they become angry or withdraw.

Warning Sign No. 31: Displaying inappropriate behavior and responses. Relapsing adolescents show a complete lack of concern for themselves or others. They do what they want and display no remorse. They may dress inappropriately in defiance, become angry or hostile in normal conversation, blame family members, and become verbally abusive and cruel.

Warning Sign No. 32: Hostile arguments and behavior at home. Hostility in a family isn't always about Mom and Dad physically abusing each other or their children. As adolescents lose control in relapse, explosive and sometimes physically threatening situations emerge. They may start physically intimidating or abusing the family. They may batter siblings or parents or threaten to do so.

Arguments with these adolescents turn into fights. They may scream cruel accusations, threaten and swear at family members. They may slam doors, turn their stereos up to the max, glare at family members, or refuse to answer when they are spoken to. These are all forms of hostile behavior.

Warning Sign No. 33: Explosive behavior at school. Because they are now so dysfunctional and believe that nobody is coming to their rescue, relapsing adolescents feel pent-up aggression, frustration, and hostility. Their problems at school have become so regular and so severe that they may now be suspended or expelled. They may get into physical fights at school with other adolescents or teachers when perhaps they have never been in fights before.

Warning Sign No. 34: Impulsive behaviors. Relapsing adolescents get involved in behaviors without thinking about the consequences. They may start doing things such as shoplifting, telling off a teacher, embarrassing their parents, taking a car for a joy ride, or staying out past curfew.

PHASE EIGHT
Recognition of Loss of Control

During Phase Eight relapsing adolescents recognize that they are losing control of their lives. They believe that they are hopeless and that recovery is impossible for them. They search for sympathetic ears to unload on and return to manipulating others. They feel that nobody has any answers for them, that nobody is offering them any help. They believe they are doing what everyone told them would put their lives back in order.

Warning Sign No. 35: Feeling self-pity and using sympathy-evoking tactics. Adolescents realize that they have contributed to their problems at school and at home, and they begin to feel sorry for themselves. "I'm out of control and nobody cares!" Some call this "P-L-O-M," poor-little-old-me. People have been distancing from them and they feel angry and frustrated by this.

Adolescents blame their illness for their behavior and search for people who will listen to how bad things are. They believe that no one will "give them a break." They feel that nobody cares or will listen to them and they are right. By this point, people are so burned up with them that their sympathy-evoking tactics no longer work.

Warning Sign No. 36: Dwelling on pretreatment experiences. Adolescents begin focusing on "war stories" and sharing stories or thoughts about drinking episodes that were fun and exciting. "How wonderful some of my highs were. Some of my drugging days were really fun." They remember how great it was to be high on chemicals and forget about all the bad things that happened as a result of their chemical use.

They think about "that great time when...," or "that one party...," or "that girl [or boy] I got high with...." They move from treatment reminiscence (dwelling on how great inpatient was) to pretreatment reminiscence (dwelling on past highs), which is a very dangerous sign.

Warning Sign No. 37: Thinking of chemical use. Adolescents begin toying with the decision to use alcohol or drugs again. They think, "I might be able to use chemicals and control it now." "I might be able to use..." because that would work. They know how to get relief when they're feeling this bad and out of control. They start entertaining the idea that they might be able to use, just for a while, just until they can get past this hump.

PHASE NINE
Option Reduction

In Phase Nine, relapsing adolescents have withdrawn from all helping systems: AA/NA, counselors, and Twelve-Step sponsors. Any attempts to reach these adolescents now seem futile. They are experiencing guilt and feelings of failure.

Warning Sign No. 38: Withdrawing from all forms of help. Adolescents refuse to resume attendance at AA/NA or aftercare meetings and avoid their counselors and AA/NA sponsors completely. When forced, their interaction with these people is short and superficial.

Warning Sign No. 39: Having major attitude change. At this point, relapsing adolescents withdraw and become complacent and quiet, interacting with others as little as possible and isolating.

PHASE TEN
Return to Alcohol or Drug Use

It isn't very long after adolescents start thinking along these lines that they are into Phase Ten. They are now in a critical condition—they are back on chemicals. At first, they try to use alcohol or drugs in a "controlled" manner, many times starting with their secondary drug of choice. For example, recovering cocaine addicts may believe they can still handle alcohol.

Adolescents experience feelings of shame and guilt over using again and need to continue using to escape from these feelings. Eventually they lose control over their chemical use. Their initial, pretreatment fears of failure have been realized. They feel guilty, helpless, and hopeless and see no way out. Their self-esteem is at an all-time low. They are too embarrassed and ashamed to ask others for help. The self-defeating behaviors they begin to engage in at this point can result in severe depression and increased drinking or drug use. They may even begin to have serious thoughts of suicide which places them in life-threatening situations. As these adolescents have progressed through the relapse process, the attention and support from those who rallied around them in their early recovery have turned into resentment and disgust, and this reinforces their feelings of worthlessness.

Possible hospital admission. Adolescents' parents may now believe that treatment has failed and may seek alternatives. They may decide to have their adolescents admitted to mental health units to relieve pressure on the family. Adolescents may also be admitted to such facilities as a result of suicide attempts or drug overdoses.

Recurrence of initial problems. Relapsing adolescents see a progressive return of all the problems which surfaced prior to their getting treatment—except now they are worse. Their previous problems and symptoms are now increased in intensity, plus they may have new problems with school, their health, or the law.

Serious accidents. In acute relapse, adolescents are at increased risk of accidents at school, at home, and especially in automobiles.

If they are relapse prone, they have an added burden of guilt, failure, disgust, and hopelessness that comes with trying and failing repeatedly at recovery. They seem to take more risks, and to care less. Also, while abstinent, their tolerance to chemicals may have dropped and they may get "blown out" when they resume drinking and using drugs.

How Can We Use These Relapse Warning Signs?

There are many opportunities to intervene in the relapse process long before adolescents actually return to chemical use. The further along in the progression of relapse they get, the more difficult it is to help them pull out of it. The earlier in the process their relapse is identified and interrupted, the quicker they can get back into working a recovery program.

One of the keys to preventing relapse is education; another is openness. Adolescents need to talk to their aftercare counselors and sponsors about their recovery and point out where they are in that process. They need to talk about what they should be working on now, where they should be going next, what they have to accomplish in recovery, and what their relapse warning signs are.

Adolescents need to communicate this to people around them who will reinforce their recovery and say, "Look, you said this is one of your warning signs, and you are acting it out."

Adolescents can learn to identify when they are in early relapse and to tell somebody about it. They can tell their sponsor or their counselor, somebody who can help them to interrupt the process. Relapse doesn't have to go all the way to chemical use.

Relapse Does Not Mean Failure

Like people who are treated for other chronic illness such as cancer, some go into remission or recovery and then periodically get very sick again. If cancer goes into remission for a while and then returns, it doesn't mean that the patient is a failure! And it doesn't mean that the medical team failed either.

If chemically dependent adolescents relapse, no matter how far this progresses, it doesn't mean that they are a failure or that their treatment program has failed. Remember, chemical dependency is a disease that is prone to relapse. It is not necessary for adolescents to relapse all the way to using chemicals again, but if they do, the most important thing is to get them back into their recovery program as soon as possible.

What to Do When a Recovering
Chemically Dependent Adolescent Relapses

When chemically dependent adolescents relapse back to chemical use, the first thing we need to do is to get them sober and physically stabilized. If there are signs of withdrawal, they may require medical supervision during detoxification. A second option to consider is readmitting them for a *temporary* stay in an inpatient program, for three to seven days. This will help to get them away from chemicals while they are stabilizing. Or they can return to an intensive outpatient program for a few weeks before going back into ongoing outpatient therapy.

The next thing that needs to be done for adolescents who were actually in recovery and then relapsed back to chemical use is to identify where they got stuck in their recovery process. Where did recovery start to go wrong for them? What issues are interfering with their ability to stay sober? Are there family problems? Is there a lack of progress in their normal adolescent development tasks? What is missing from their treatment plans, in terms of managing their recovery?

We have to find the specific reasons why these adolescents relapsed. Perhaps a dual diagnosis was present and missed the first time through treatment and is interfering with the child's ability to stay sober. Once these have been identified, then we have to focus on helping adolescents deal with the problems that are interfering with their recovery. This may mean that additional therapy is needed or some specific one-on-one work.

If adolescents have problems staying sober, it is important to look at getting them involved in **relapse prevention therapy.** This model of treatment is focused around identifying personal relapse warning signs and professional relapse prevention therapy. There are certified relapse prevention therapists throughout the country who can help relapse-prone chemically dependent adolescents.

It is important to identify what started to move them away from stable recovery. What was the first thing that went wrong and started them into a relapse process? Also, what relapse warning signs did they experience as they were becoming dysfunctional? These things have to be identified in order to prevent these problems from occurring again and sabotaging these adolescents' future attempts at recovery.

A Message for Families

Most families of chemically dependent adolescents will rally around their newly recovering youngsters. They go to Al-Anon meetings and to family education meetings. Adolescents will have AA/NA sponsors, go to support groups and aftercare, and everything will seem to be going well.

If adolescents go through periods of relapse that end in chemical use, quite often everybody jumps ship; everybody shuts them down. Parents say, "I give up. That's it. See what we did? We invested all this time and energy into this adolescent and there he is out using again."

Many times they literally turn their backs on adolescents who relapse. It's as if they are saying, "One chance, that's all you get. I invested my time and energy and you failed. I'm done with you." That is a common response. It is also a co-dependent response. What the family members are saying is, "I'm taking this kid's relapse personally. He's not responding the way he should have, and that's what I need from him because of all I did for him. He did this to me!" That is the statement that's often made to the relapsed adolescent.

Chemically dependent adolescents who relapse are not bad; they are sick. They need you now more than ever.

Each family member needs to continue to focus on his or her own recovery regardless of whether the chemically dependent adolescent progresses in recovery or back into relapse. The important thing for the family to do is to get well for the benefit of each member in it and to be there to encourage the adolescent to try again.

Chemically dependent adolescents who relapse are not bad; they are sick. They need us more than ever once they've relapsed. They need you now more than ever.

Note: The "Adolescent Relapse Warning Signs" were adapted from *The Phases and Warning Signs of Alcoholic Relapse,* by Terence T. Gorski (Independence, Mo.: Herald House/Independence Press).

Chapter
8

Final Words to Parents

If, after being fully evaluated by a chemical dependency specialist, your child is diagnosed as chemically dependent, you will need to make some important decisions regarding appropriate treatment. I want to emphasize the necessity for your adolescent to complete the pretreatment tasks described in detail in Chapter 6 as an outpatient *if* possible, prior to being admitted to an inpatient treatment program. Allow the chemical dependency specialist to guide you here. In emergencies, immediate hospitalization is necessary.

Pretreatment includes processes that help adolescents recognize (1) that they have a significant problem with chemical use; (2) that they cannot control their use; and (3) that they need help with this problem. Selecting the right treatment program for adolescents will (1) provide them with the best chance to recover from their illness, and (2) provide the help you need to recover as individuals and as a family.

There are numerous programs treating adolescent chemical dependency that are doing marvelous therapy with adolescents. Unfortunately there are also treatment programs that aren't very effective. I hope to help you avoid the less effective programs.

Check out these basic criteria that treatment facilities

173

should meet regardless of their credibility, their experience, or their good reputation in treating *adult* chemical dependence before you decide to admit your adolescent for inpatient treatment.

What to Look for in a Treatment Center

A good quality facility for treatment of adolescent chemical dependency will have the following ten components:
1. *Assessment and stabilization procedures*
2. *An academic program*
3. *Drug and alcohol education*
4. *Group and individual therapy*
5. *Treatment planning*
6. *Exercise, recreation, proper nutrition, and stress management*
7. *A comprehensive family program*
8. *Intensive outpatient aftercare*
9. *Twelve-Step approach*
10. *Relapse prevention therapy*

---

1. *Assessment procedures* means the ability to make clinical observation and use objective tests. This must be done by a professional staff person with expertise in addiction. The clinician should be able to evaluate an adolescent on three levels: (1) where the child is in respect to normal adolescent development; (2) whether or not there is evidence of a dual diagnosis (meaning the adolescent is affected by conditions other than chemical dependency); and (3) accurately describe the adolescent's chemical dependence, including primary and secondary drugs of choice.

Stabilization procedures means (1) providing medical detoxification if necessary for adolescents who experience symptoms of physical withdrawal; (2) taking a complete medical history, including a comprehensive physical examination; (3) a plan for orienting the incoming adolescent to the facility; and (4) professional intervention personnel to counsel adolescents about the crisis that brought them to treatment.

2. *An academic program* should be designed to (1) assist adolescents with current school assignments and (2) assess adolescents for possible learning disabilities.

3. *Drug and alcohol education* should be designed to teach adolescents about chemical dependence, recovery, and relapse prevention.

4. *Group and individual therapy* needs to be (1) structured and (2) problem-focused. Ask how adolescent groups are conducted, what the goals of group therapy are, and how progress in the group process is monitored. Individual therapy should be available to adolescents at least twice a week.

5. *Treatment planning* does not mean a generalized overview of the assessment process. Find out what specific problems are on *your* adolescent's treatment plan and how the therapist determined them. Most important, find out how the program's therapists plan to help the adolescent resolve these problems.

6. *Exercise, recreation, nutrition, and stress management* means a holistic health approach. Part of recovery is feeling well. Make sure that the program provides for and stresses exercise, recreation, good nutrition, and stress management.

7. *A comprehensive family program* consists of education about chemical dependence and codependence for adolescents' families. It should conduct family therapy with the adolescent and the family and require that family members

participate in Al-Anon or NarAnon.

8. *Intensive outpatient aftercare* is essential. Make sure that a structured outpatient program for both the chemically dependent adolescent and the family is available. A once-a-week aftercare group for twelve weeks is insufficient. Immediately following discharge from treatment, the program should provide or refer you to long-term outpatient therapy that is structured to provide support for one to two years.

9. *Twelve-Step approach* means the facility subscribes to Twelve-Step programs such as Alcoholics Anonymous (AA), Narcotics Anonymous (NA), Cocaine Anonymous (CA), etc. Make sure that the program not only endorses Twelve-Step principles and participation but that it involve the adolescent in Twelve-Step meetings during treatment.

10. *Relapse prevention* means that a relapse prevention plan is developed for the chemically dependent adolescent prior to discharge. This plan should include (1) listing the adolescent's personal relapse warning signs; (2) developing management strategies for these warning signs; and (3) identifying the adolescent's future high-risk situations.

Treatment Programs to Avoid

There are treatment programs which practice policies or procedures that will not serve to help your adolescent and which may do harm. Ask questions about the programs you may be considering and avoid them if they include the following treatment approaches and practices.

1. *Do not subscribe to a Twelve-Step philosophy* or do not provide opportunities for adolescents to attend Twelve-Step meetings.

2. *Mix adolescents with adults.* This has not been effective. Adolescents are not supposed to behave as adults, yet adult patients become frustrated when adolescents act

like children. Both staff and adult patients in treatment tend to parent adolescents, and codependent relationships frequently develop.

Adolescents require a specialized body of knowledge and the program content should reflect this. However, when adolescents are both eighteen years old and out of school, they should be placed in treatment with adults because that is now their peer group.

3. *Claim an 80-90 percent success rate.* This simply is not happening. I have personally followed up on many such claims and none of them have been valid. Sometimes it means only that adolescents are drug-free at discharge! Beware of programs that make such claims.

4. *Are punitive in nature.* This includes programs that allow staff to physically punish adolescents, have harsh restrictions, or let group members punish each other, physically or emotionally. Let your instincts guide you. If any behavior or practice in the program seems weird or bizarre, it probably is.

5. *Are ambiguous about what they do.* Sound programs apply well-developed, standard methods for treating chemically dependent adolescents. They do not leave parents in the dark.

No treatment center can promise a cure for chemical dependency, and no ethical one will. Proper inpatient treatment *can* provide your adolescent with knowledge and with a foundation in sobriety on which to build a stable recovery program. Your active participation in the treatment phase of your adolescent's recovery process will help you to recognize both problems that will develop and the progress your adolescent makes.

As parents, your participation begins in obtaining accurate information about the disease and treatment of chemical dependence from professionals qualified to deal with the special needs of adolescents. The need for your participation does not end with your adolescent's "graduation" from a treatment program. The road to recovery involves time, effort, and—what is most important—your understanding of difficult tasks and challenges that your adolescent will have to face in the recovery process.

The need for your participation does not end with your adolescent's graduation from a treatment program.

Perhaps the best way to learn what adolescents must learn to do differently, how you can best help them, and how they feel about what lies ahead for them is to hear it from them.

A Letter to Mom and Dad

Dear Mom and Dad,

I'm writing this to you because I want to explain some things that I can't bring myself to say to you face-to-face. I'm scared and ashamed to admit this to you, but here goes.

First of all I'm really sorry you got me for your kid—I know I'm less than you hoped for. I'm sorry for all the bad things I've done to you and to myself. I've tricked you, I've lied to you and used you. I'm sorry I'm chemically dependent. I hope you can forgive me for the pain and embarrassment I've caused you. Most of all I'm sorry that all I can do is say I'm sorry.

Believe it or not, I felt bad about the things I did to you even as I was doing them. I just couldn't stop myself. The more I did and got away with, the easier it got.

I know it's no excuse, but I've never felt I was "good"

enough. I never seem to fit in anywhere, especially at school, and it hurts. I know you don't think it's important that I fit in but it's very important to me.

When I started using drugs I could escape from the pain of not being good enough. I felt like I fit in for the first time. Drug users accepted me because I used drugs, and unfortunately doing drugs was something I could do. I never meant for it to go this far. I didn't realize it could.

I've always blamed myself for all the problems in our family, including the problems between the two of you. Do you realize our family isn't normal? Why can't we act like we love each other? Why can't we stop fighting? Why can't we talk to each other and why can't we just have some fun? We all act miserable, like we hardly know each other. God, I hate that. I want us to be a family. I just wish that life wasn't so hard, and so painful and confusing.

As I try to recover from my addiction, I'm really scared of failing you and myself again. There are some things I need from you to help me make it.

Please listen to me about the things that are important to me, and try to act like what I'm saying is important to you, too, and not stupid kid stuff.

Try to trust me. I'm not saying let me walk all over you or use you; I know enabling hurts me. I mean just give me another chance.

Help me grow up; I hate being a teenager. I want to grow up, and I will grow up. And I need you to let me learn some things on my own.

Talk to me about the way you see things or the way you learned about things, but please don't *lecture* me, or threaten me or scream at me. It doesn't work. I like to know what your opinions are, but sometimes I just need for you to listen to me without getting mad or criticizing me or telling me what to do. I'm trying to learn to make my own decisions.

Please support me in my recovery. Please make it important to you. I need for you to take it seriously. Don't complain about driving me to AA/NA meetings or about having to attend counseling sessions. Don't complain about paying for treatment; it makes me feel guilty and worthless.

Please don't run down my counselors to me. I need to believe in them if I'm going to make it. Don't help me come up with excuses for not doing what they tell me to do, and don't make it easy for me to get discouraged or to quit trying. It's easy for me to give up on myself.

If I have problems in my recovery or if I relapse like so many other kids, don't give up on me. I don't do things to *you*—I do things to *me*.

I want you to take care of yourselves and each other so you'll both be strong enough to get behind me when I have to have your help again, because I know I will. I have a disease, Mom and Dad, and it won't ever go away. Help me get better; stand behind me as I learn how to recover from this and how to become an adult. Please try to keep loving me until I can learn how to love myself. I need you.

Love,

Your Chemically Dependent Kid

Bibliography

Ackerman, Robert J. *Children of Alcoholics: A Guide for Educators, Therapists, and Parents.* Holmes Beach, Florida: Learning Publications, 1978.

"Alcohol Tolerance Different in COA Men," a news story in *U.S. Journal of Drug and Alcohol Dependence,* vol. 9, no. 12 (December 1985): 12.

Alcoholics Anonymous. New York: Alcoholics Anonymous World Services, Inc., 1955.

Barun, Ken. *When Saying No Isn't Enough.* New York: The Atlantic Monthly Press, 1989.

Bell, Tammy L. *Adolescent Relapse Warning Signs.* Independence, Missouri: Herald House/Independence Press, 1989.

_____. "Can We Promise to Do No Harm?" *Professional Counselor* (November/December 1989).

_____. "Motivating Adolescents to Accept Treatment" *Alcoholism & Addiction & Recovery* (November 1989).

_____. "Relapse Isn't the End of the World," *Adolescent Counselor* (October/November 1989).

_____. "Understanding Adolescent Chemical Dependence" (audiotape series). Independence, Missouri: Herald House/Independence Press, 1989.

Berger, Kathleen. *The Developing Person.* New York: Worth Publishers, Inc., 1980.

Berne, Patricia H., and Louis M. Savary. *Building Self-Esteem in Children.* New York: The Continuum Publishing Company, 1987.

Bill B. *Compulsive Overeater: The Basic Text for Compulsive Overeaters.* Minneapolis, Minnesota: Comp Care Publications, 1981.

Black, Claudia. *It Will Never Happen to Me.* Denver: MAC Printing and Publishing Division, 1982.

Brown, Stephanie. *Treating the Alcoholic: A Developmental Model of Recovery.* New York: John Wiley & Sons, 1985.

Daley, Dennis C., Havard Moss, and Francis Campbell. *Dual-Disorders—Counseling Clients with Chemical Dependency and Mental Illness.* Center City, Minnesota: The Hazelden Foundation, 1987.

Defining Adolescent Alcohol Use. Washington, D.C.: National Council on Alcoholism, 1977.

Diagnostic and Statistical Manual of Mental Disorders, Third Edition (revised). Washington, D.C.: American Psychiatric Association, 1987.

Dittl, James A. "Relapse and SAP Recovery Groups," *Student Assistance Journal* (November/December 1988).

Ellis, Dan C. *Growing Up Stoned.* Pompano Beach, Florida: Health Communications, Inc., 1986.

Gitlow, Stanley E., and Herbert S. Peyser. *Alcoholism: A Practical Treatment Guide.* New York: Grune & Stratton, 1980.

Glenn, Stephen H., and Joel W. Warner. *Developing Capable Young People.* Texas: Humansphere, 1982.

Glenn, Stephen. *Raising Children for Success: Blue Prints and Building Blocks for Developing Capable People.* Fair Oaks, California: Sunrise Press, 1987.

Goodwin, Donald. *Is Alcoholism Hereditary?* New York: Oxford University Press, 1976.

Gorski, Terence T. *Denial Patterns: A System for Understanding the Alcoholic's Behavior.* Harvey, Illinois: Ingalls Memorial Hospital, 1976 (available from the CENAPS Corporation, P.O. Box 184, Hazel Crest, IL 60429).

_____. *Passages Through Recovery.* New York: A Harper-Hazelden Book, The Hazelden Foundation, 1989.

_____. *The Dynamics of Relapse in the Alcoholic Patient.* Harvey, Illinois: Ingalls Memorial Hospital, 1976.

_____. *The Relapse/Recovery Grid.* Center City, Minn.: Hazelden Educational Materials, 1989.

_____. *The Staying Sober Workbook: A Serious Solution for the Problem of Relapse.* Independence, Missouri: Herald House/Independence Press, 1988.

_____. *The Twelve Steps: A Guide for Counselors and Therapists.* Independence, Missouri: Herald House/Independence Press, 1989.

Gorski, Terence T., and Merlene Miller. *The Phases and Warning Signs of Relapse.* Independence, Missouri: Herald House/Independence Press, 1984.

_____. *Counseling for Relapse Prevention.* Independence, Missouri: Herald House/Independence Press, 1982.

_____. *Staying Sober: A Guide for Relapse Prevention.* Independence, Missouri: Herald House/Independence Press, 1986.

Harrison, Patricia Ann, and Norman G. Hoffmann. *CATOR 1989—Adolescent Residential Treatment Intake and Follow-up Findings.* St. Paul, Minn.: Ramsey Clinic, 1989.

Havighurst, Robert J. *Developmental Tasks and Education.* New York: David McKay Company, Inc., 1952 (revised 1965).

Henry, Paul B. *Adolescent Chemical Dependency—A Guide to Clinical Assessment and Intervention.* New York: The Hayworth Press, 1989.

Heuer, Marti. *Happy Daze.* Denver: M.A.C., 1986.

Hollis, Judi. *Fat Is a Family Affair.* Center City, Minn.: The Hazelden Foundation, 1985.

Hsu, George L.K., and Michel Hersen. *Recent Developments in Adolescent Psychiatry.* New York: John Wiley & Sons, 1989.

Jellinek, E. M. *The Disease Concept of Alcoholism.* New Haven, Conn.: College and University Press in association with Hillhouse Press (New Brunswick, N.J.), 1960.

Johnson, Vernon E. *I'll Quit Tomorrow.* New York: Harper & Row, 1973.

Ketcham, Katherine, and L. Ann Mueller. *Eating Right to Live Sober.* Seattle, Washington: Madrona Publishers, 1981.

Kinney, Jean, and Gwen Leaton. *Loosening the Grip.* St. Louis, Missouri: C.V. Mosby Co., 1978.

Levenkron, Steven. *Treating and Overcoming Anorexia Nervosa.* New York: Warner Books, 1982.

Marlatt, G. A. "Craving for Alcohol, Loss of Control, and Relapse: A Cognitive Behavioral Analysis," in P.E. Nathan, T.A. Marlatt, and T. Robers (eds.), *Behavioral Research and Treatment.* New York: Plenum, 1978.

_____. "Relapse Prevention: Theoretical Rationale and Overview of the Model," in G. Alan Marlatt and Judith R. Gordon(eds.), *Relapse Prevention—Maintenance Strategies in the Treatment of Addictive Behaviors.* New York: The Guilford Press, 1985: 3-70.

Milam, James, and Katherine Ketcham. *Under the Influence—A Guide to the Myths and Realities of Alcoholism.* Seattle, Washington: Madrona Publishers, 1981.

Miller, Alice. *The Dream of the Gifted Child.* New York: Basic Books, Inc., 1981.

Miller, Merlene, and Terence T. Gorski. *Family Recovery: Growing Beyond Addiction.* Independence, Missouri: Herald House/Independence Press, 1982.

Narcotics Anonymous World Service Office, Inc. *Narcotics Anonymous.* New York: C.A.R.E.N.A. Publishing Company, 1982.

National Institute on Drug Abuse. *Drug Use Among American High School Students, College Students, and Other Young Adults: National Trends through 1985* (DDHS Publication No. ADM 86-1450). Washington, D.C.: U.S. Government Printing Office, 1986.

Pearce, Joseph Chilton. *Magical Child.* New York: Bantam Books, 1986.

_____. *Magical Child Matures.* New York: Bantam Books, 1986.

Perkins, William Mack, and Nancy McMurtie-Perkins. *Raising Drug Free Kids in a Drug Filled World.* Center City, Minn.: The Hazelden Foundation, 1986.

Schell, Robert E., and Elizabeth Hall. *Developmental Psychology Today.* New York: Random House, 1979.

Siepker, Barbara B. (A.M.), and Christine S. Kandaras (A.M.). *Group Therapy with Children and Adolescents.* New York: Human Sciences Press, Inc., 1985.

Stein, Michael D., and J. Kent Davis. *Therapies for Adolescents.* San Francisco: Jossey-Bass Publisher, 1985.

Stone, Joseph, and Joseph Church. *Childhood and Adolescence.* New York: Random House, 1973.

Twelve Steps and Twelve Traditions. New York: Alcoholics Anonymous Publishing, Inc. (now known as A.A. World Services, Inc.), 1957.

Vaillant, George E. *The Natural History of Alcoholism: Causes, Patterns, and Paths to Recovery.* Cambridge, Mass.: Harvard University Press, 1983.

Weedman, Richard D., and William E. Stone. *Effective Treatment for Adolescent Chemical Abuse and Dependency.* Irvine, California: National Association of Alcoholism Treatment Program, Inc., 1986.

Wegsheider, Sharon. *Another Chance—Hope and Health for the Alcoholic Family.* Palo Alto, California: Science and Behavior Books, Inc., 1983.

Woititz, Janet Geringer. *Adult Children of Alcoholics.* Pompano Beach, Florida: Health Communications, Inc., 1985.

Yoder, Jean (M.D.), and William Proctor. *The Self-Confident Child.* New York: Facts on File Publications, 1988.